Weekend Scrap
Quilting™

Edited by Jeanne Stauffer and Sandra L. Hatch

HOUSE of
WHITE
BIRCHES

PUBLISHERS
SINCE 1947

WEEKEND SCRAP QUILTING

EDITORS	Jeanne Stauffer, Sandra L. Hatch
ART DIRECTOR	Brad Snow
PUBLISHING SERVICES MANAGER	Brenda Gallmeyer
ASSOCIATE EDITOR	Dianne Schmidt
ASSISTANT ART DIRECTOR	Karen Allen
COPY SUPERVISOR	Michelle Beck
COPY EDITORS	Conor Allen, Sue Harvey, Nicki Lehman
TECHNICAL ARTIST	Connie Rand
GRAPHIC PRODUCTION SUPERVISOR	Ronda Bechinski
BOOK DESIGN	Edith Teegarden
GRAPHIC ARTIST	Glenda Chamberlain
PRODUCTION ASSISTANTS	Cheryl Kempf, Marj Morgan
PHOTOGRAPHY	Tammy Christian, Christena Green, Kelly Wiard
PHOTO STYLIST	Tammy Nussbaum
CHIEF EXECUTIVE OFFICER	John Robinson
PUBLISHING DIRECTOR	David J. McKee
EDITORIAL DIRECTOR	Vivian Rothe
BOOK MARKETING DIRECTOR	Craig Scott

Printed in the United States of America
First Printing: 2004
Library of Congress Number: 2004105975
ISBN: 1-59217-050-1

1 2 3 4 5 6 7 8 9

Welcome

There are two kinds of quilts that every quilter we know likes to make: scrap quilts and weekend quilts. They all like to make scrap quilts because it gives them the opportunity to use all those too-gorgeous-to-pass-up fabrics that they purchased without any idea of where they would be used. Or, they love making scrap quilts because it reduces the size of their stash and gives them the opportunity to buy even more fabric.

The second kind of quilt that every quilter we know loves to make is a weekend quilt. By a weekend quilt, we are referring to a quilt that is so easy to make that you can complete the quilt top from start to finish in a weekend or two. If you use machine piecing and machine appliqué, you can finish every one of the quilt tops in this book in 20 hours. Most of them can be made in much less time than that.

So *Weekend Scrap Quilting* has the best of both worlds. There are 35 quilts in this book; all are scrappy and all can be made in a weekend or two. It doesn't get any better than this! So what are you waiting for? Open these pages and start planning your weekends. There isn't a better way to spend a weekend than quilting. You don't even need to go shopping first. Pull out your stash and start planning your first weekend scrap quilt. You'll enjoy every stitch and every minute of the weekend!

Warm regards,

Jeanne Stauffer

Sandra L. Hatch

Contents

ANIMAL LOG CABIN
11½" x 11½" Block

CORNER LOG CABIN
5" x 5" Block

Embroidered Blocks Baby Quilt

DESIGN > PAULA JEFFERY

Lots of 1930s-looking scraps make the Log Cabin blocks in this pieced-and-embroidered baby quilt.

PROJECT SPECIFICATIONS

Skill Level: Beginner
Quilt Size: 34½" x 34½"
Block Size: 11½" and 5"
Number of Blocks: 4 each size

MATERIALS

- 4 (6" x 6") white tonal A squares
- Assorted 2"-wide strips for log pieces
- Assorted 1½"-wide strips for log pieces
- ⅓ yard blue print for binding
- ¾ yard salmon solid
- Backing 40" x 40"
- Batting 40" x 40"
- Neutral color all-purpose thread
- Quilting thread
- Salmon 6-strand embroidery floss
- Basic sewing tools and supplies

INSTRUCTIONS

Step 1. Transfer the embroidery designs given to the A squares.

Step 2. Using 3 strands salmon embroidery floss, stem-stitch along marked lines. Make French knots for eyes.

Step 3. To make Animal Log Cabin blocks, cut four scrap strips each 2" x 6" (piece 1) and 12" x 12" (piece 8).

Step 4. Cut eight scrap strips each 2" x 7½" (pieces 2 and 3), 2" x 9" (pieces 4 and 5) and 2" x 10½" (pieces 6 and 7).

Step 5. Sew pieces to an embroidered A square in numerical order referring to **Figure 1**; press seams

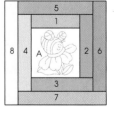

FIGURE 1 Sew pieces to A in numerical order to make Animal Log Cabin blocks.

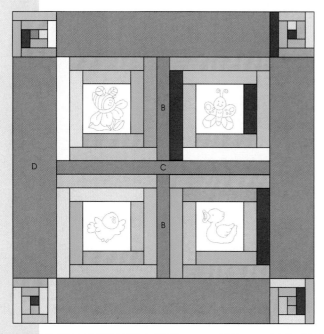

EMBROIDERED BLOCKS BABY QUILT Placement Diagram 34½" x 34½"

toward strips. Repeat to make four Animal Log Cabin blocks.

Step 6. To make Corner Log Cabin blocks, cut eight 1½" x 1½" scrap squares for pieces 1 and 2.

Step 7. Cut eight scrap strips each 1½" x 2½" (pieces 3 and 4), 1½" x 3½" (pieces 5 and 6) and 1½" x 4½" (pieces 7 and 8), and four scrap strips 1½" x 5½" (piece 9).

Step 8. Sew pieces together in numerical order as shown in **Figure 2**; press seams toward strips. Repeat to make four Corner Log Cabin blocks.

FIGURE 2 Sew pieces in numerical order to make Corner Log Cabin blocks.

Step 9. Cut two 2" x 12" B strips and one 2" x 25" C strips salmon solid along length of fabric.

Step 10. Join two blocks with a B strip; press seams toward B. Repeat for two rows.

Step 11. Join the pieced rows with the C strip; press seams toward C.

Step 12. Cut four 5½" x 25" D strips salmon solid along length of fabric.

Step 13. Sew a D strip to opposite sides of the pieced center; press seams toward D.

Step 14. Sew a Corner Log Cabin block to each end of the remaining D strips; press seams toward D.

Step 15. Sew a strip to the remaining sides of the pieced center to complete the pieced top.

BEE EMBROIDERY DESIGN

Step 16. Sandwich the batting between the completed top and prepared backing; pin or baste layers together to hold.

Step 17. Hand- or machine-quilt as desired. When quilting is complete, trim batting and backing even with top; remove pins or basting.

Step 18. Cut four 2¼" by fabric width strips blue print for binding. Join strips on short ends to make one long strip. Fold the strip in half along length with wrong sides together; press.

Step 19. Sew binding to quilt edges, mitering corners and overlapping ends. Fold binding to the backside and stitch in place to finish. ◆

DUCK EMBROIDERY DESIGN

BIRD EMBROIDERY DESIGN

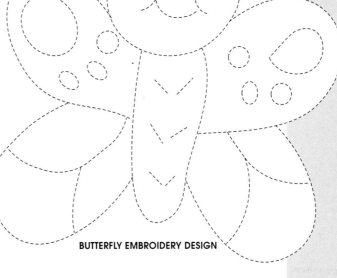

BUTTERFLY EMBROIDERY DESIGN

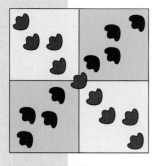

LARGE FOOTPRINT
14" x 14" Block

DINOSAUR
14" x 9" Block

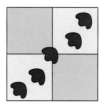

SMALL FOOTPRINT
9" x 9" Block

My Dinosaur
Baby

DESIGN > BARBARA CLAYTON

Dinosaur footprints trail across this pretty baby quilt.

PROJECT SPECIFICATIONS

Skill Level: Intermediate
Quilt Size: 42" x 42" without prairie points
Block Size: 14" x 9", 9" x 9" and 14" x 14"
Number of Blocks: 4, 4 and 1

MATERIALS

- Scrap dark green tonal
- ¼ yard green mottled
- ½ yard lime green mottled
- ½ yard bright purple tonal
- ⅔ yard medium purple mottled
- ⅔ yard dark purple mottled
- ¾ yard turquoise mottled
- 1 yard yellow mottled
- Backing 48" x 48"
- Batting 48" x 48"
- Neutral color and black all-purpose thread
- Clear nylon monofilament
- Quilting thread
- ¼ yard fusible web
- 1 yard fusible interfacing
- Stylet, knitting needle or pencil with broken lead
- Basic tools and supplies

INSTRUCTIONS

Cutting

Step 1. Cut four 14½" x 9½" A rectangles yellow mottled.

Step 2. Cut eight squares each yellow (B) and lime green (C) mottleds 5" x 5".

Step 3. Cut two squares each yellow (D) and lime green (E) mottleds 7½" x 7½".

Step 4. Cut four 3" by fabric width strips turquoise mottled; subcut into (16) 9½" F strips.

Step 5. Cut two 3" by fabric width strips green mottled; subcut into (16) 3" G squares.

Step 6. Cut four 3" by fabric width strips turquoise mottled; subcut into eight 14½" H strips.

Step 7. Cut three 2" by fabric width strips dark purple mottled; subcut into (56) 2" I squares.

Step 8. Cut four 3½" by fabric width strips each medium (J) and dark purple (K) mottleds; subcut strips into (42) each 3½" J and K squares.

Making Dinosaur Blocks

Step 1. Fold and crease each A rectangle to mark the centers.

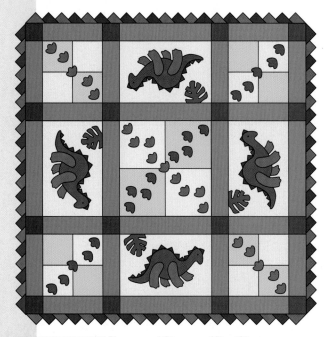

MY DINOSAUR BABY Placement Diagram 42" x 42"
(without prairie points)

Step 2. Trace the dinosaur body parts and leaf shapes onto the smooth side of the fusible interfacing referring to the patterns for number to cut. *Note: Patterns are given in reverse for fusible appliqué.*

Step 3. Cut out interfacing shapes leaving at least a ¼" margin all around. Pin the interfacing shapes with fusible side on the right side of fabrics as directed on patterns for color. Cut out shapes, leaving a margin all around.

Step 4. Stitch all around each shape except on the ends of the underneath legs and the straight edge of the leaf shapes. Trim away excess fabric close to stitching; clip curves and trim points.

Step 5. Cut a small slit in the center of the interfacing side of each shape except underneath legs and leaves as shown in **Figure 1**; turn right side out.

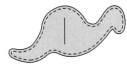

FIGURE 1 Cut a small slit in the center
of the interfacing side of each shape.

Step 6. Smooth seam edges using the stylet, knitting needle or pencil with broken lead.

Step 7. Fold each I square in half on one diagonal with wrong sides together; fold in half again to form a prairie point as shown in **Figure 2**; repeat for 56 I prairie points.

FIGURE 2 Make prairie points
as shown.

Step 8. Pin 14 I pieces to the top edge of each dinosaur from the tip of the tail to the top of the head referring to the pattern for placement suggestions. ***Note:*** *The I pieces should extend behind the dinosaur shape ¼" to ½" and are overlapped as necessary to fit.* Machine-baste I pieces in place.

Step 9. Center and fuse a dinosaur motif on each A referring to the full-size motif for order of appliqué. *Note: Forward legs are 1½" from the bottom edge and the tip of the tail is 1½" from the left side edge.*

Step 10. Using clear nylon monofilament and a narrow blind-hem stitch, sew all the way around the dinosaur shape, leaving the I pieces unstitched to the background. Stitch the top part of the legs.

Step 11. Place a leaf shape with the raw open edge even with the edge of A and 1½" from the left top corner; stitch in place as for dinosaur.

Step 12. Using black thread, drop the feed dogs for free-motion sewing and use a close, narrow zigzag stitch to sew a circle shape for the eye; fill in eye with zigzag stitches to finish the blocks.

Making Footprint Blocks

Step 1. Trace the footprint pattern onto the paper side of the fusible web as directed on pattern for number to cut. Cut out shapes, leaving a margin around each one.

Step 2. Fuse paper shapes to the wrong side of fabrics as directed on patterns for color; cut out shapes on traced lines. Remove paper backing.

Step 3. To make Small Footprint blocks, sew a B square to a C square; repeat for two B-C units. Press seams toward C. Join the B-C units to complete one block as shown in **Figure 3**; press seam in one direction. Repeat for four Small Footprint blocks.

FIGURE 3 Join the B-C units to complete 1 block.

Step 4. Repeat Step 3 with D and E squares to complete one Large Footprint block.

Step 5. Arrange four bright purple tonal footprints on each E and four medium purple mottled footprints on each D and one medium purple mottled in the block center of the Large Footprint block referring to the Placement Diagram for positioning of footprints; fuse in place.

Step 6. Arrange five bright purple tonal footprints on the B squares in two Small Footprint blocks and five medium purple mottled footprints on the C squares in the remaining two Small Footprint blocks. Stitch in place referring to Step 10 in Making Dinosaur Blocks.

Completing the Top

Step 1. Join two Small Footprint blocks with one Dinosaur block and four F strips to make a row as shown in **Figure 4**; press seams toward F. Repeat for two rows.

FIGURE 4 Join 2 Small Footprint blocks with 1 Dinosaur block and 4 F strips to make a row.

Step 2. Join two Dinosaur blocks with the Large Footprint block and four H strips to make a row as shown in **Figure 5**; press seams toward H.

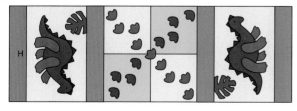

FIGURE 5 Join 2 Dinosaur blocks with the Large Footprint block and 4 H strips to make a row.

Step 3. Join four G squares with one H strip and two F strips to make a sashing row referring to **Figure 6**; press seams toward G.

G	F		H		

FIGURE 6 Join 4 G squares with 1 H strip and 2 F strips to make a sashing row.

Step 4. Join the block rows with the sashing rows to complete the pieced top; press seams toward sashing rows.

Step 5. Fold each J and K square to make prairie points referring to Step 7 for Making Dinosaur Blocks.

Step 6. Pin 10 J and 11 K units to two opposite sides and 11 J and 10 K units to the remaining sides of the completed center referring to the Placement Diagram, overlapping as necessary to fit; machine-baste to hold.

Completing the Quilt

Step 1. Lay the batting piece on a flat surface with the backing piece right side up. Pin the completed top right sides together with the backing with the prairie points between.

Step 2. Sew all around the outside edge, leaving a 6" opening along one end; trim batting and backing even with quilt top, clip corners and turn right side out through opening.

Step 3. Turn edge of opening to the inside; press the entire top flat. Hand-stitch the opening closed.

Step 4. Quilt as desired by hand or machine. ◆

FOOTPRINT
Cut 18 bright
purple tonal & 19
medium purple
mottled

LEAF
Cut 4 dark green tonal

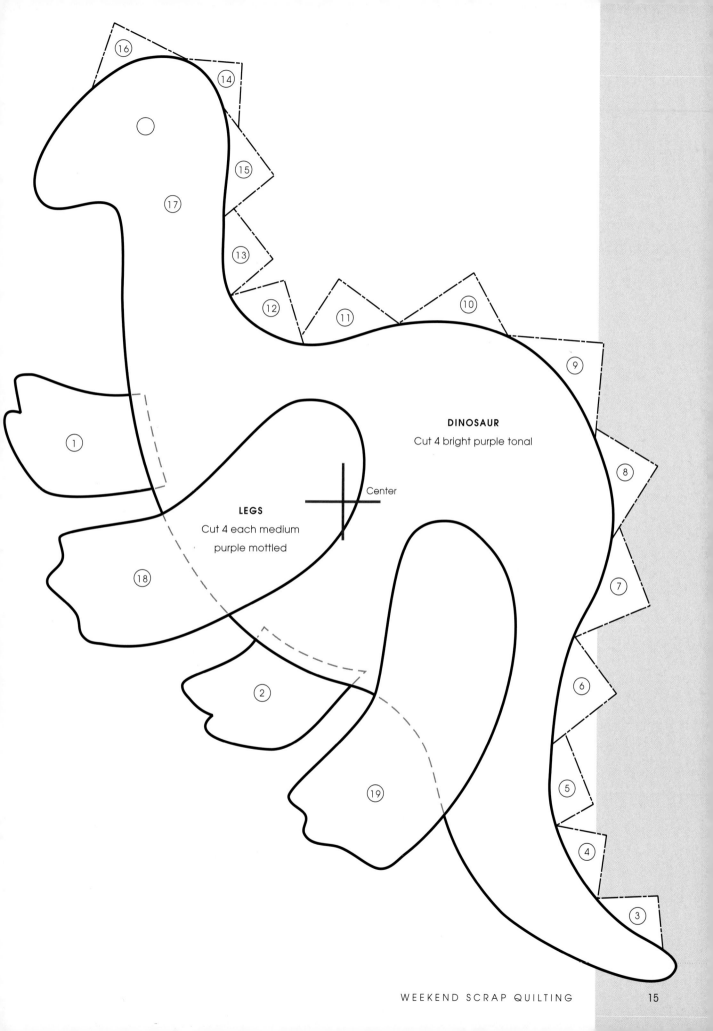

DINOSAUR
Cut 4 bright purple tonal

LEGS
Cut 4 each medium
purple mottled

Center

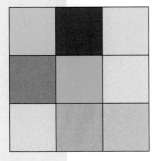

NINE-PATCH
6" x 6" Block

APPLIQUÉ BLOCK
6" x 6" Block

Farm Animal Baby Quilt

DESIGN > CHRIS MALONE

Reproduction prints create a pretty baby quilt in a style

Grandmother would love.

PROJECT SPECIFICATIONS

Skill Level: Beginner
Quilt Size: 25" x 49"
Block Size: 6" x 6"
Number of Blocks: 21

MATERIALS

- Assorted 1930s reproduction pink, blue, green yellow and red scraps
- Dark green solid scrap for appliqué
- ¼ yard blue solid
- ⅓ yard green print for binding
- ⅜ yard muslin
- ½ yard pink print
- Backing 31" x 55"
- Batting 31" x 55"
- Neutral color and black all-purpose thread
- Quilting thread
- Black 6-strand embroidery floss
- ½ yard fusible web
- ¾ yard fabric stabilizer
- Basic sewing tools and supplies

INSTRUCTIONS
Cutting

Step 1. Prepare templates for appliqué shapes using full-size patterns given. *Note: Patterns are given in reverse for fusible appliqué.*

Step 2. Trace shapes as directed onto the paper side of the fusible web. Cut out shapes, leaving a margin around each one.

Step 3. Fuse shapes to the wrong side of scrap fabrics as directed on each piece for color. Cut out shapes on traced lines; remove paper backing.

Step 4. Cut 10 muslin A squares 6½" x 6½".

Step 5. Cut 10 squares fabric stabilizer 6½" x 6½".

Step 6. Cut 99 scrap B squares 2½" x 2½".

Step 7. Cut two 1¼" x 42½" C strips and two 1¼" x 20" D strips blue solid.

Step 8. Cut (and piece) two 3¼" x 44" E strips and two 3¼" x 25½" F strips pink print.

Step 9. Cut four 2¼" by fabric width strips green print for binding.

Completing Appliqué Blocks

Step 1. Fold A squares in quarters and lightly press to mark centers. Center one appliqué motif on each A square; fuse shapes in place in numerical order.

Step 2. Pin a fabric stabilizer square behind each fused square.

Step 3. Machine blanket-stitch around each shape using black all-purpose thread; remove fabric stabilizer.

Step 4. Using 2 strands black embroidery floss, stem-stitch detail lines and make straight-stitch X's for eyes.

Completing Nine-Patch Blocks

Step 1. Select nine different B squares. Join three squares to make a row; press seams in one direction. Repeat for three rows.

Step 2. Join the rows with seams of adjacent rows going in opposite directions to complete one Nine-Patch block as shown in **Figure 1**; repeat for 11 blocks.

FIGURE 1 Join B squares to make a Nine-Patch block.

Completing the Top

Step 1. Arrange Nine-Patch blocks with Appliqué blocks in seven rows of three blocks each referring to the Placement Diagram for positioning of blocks.

Step 2. Join blocks in rows; press seams of adjacent rows in opposite directions. Join rows to complete the pieced center; press seams in one direction.

Step 3. Sew a C strip to opposite long sides and D strips to the top and bottom of the pieced center; press seams toward strips.

Step 4. Sew an E strip to opposite long sides and F strips to the top and bottom of the pieced center; press seams toward strips.

Finishing the Quilt

Step 1. Sandwich the batting between the completed top and prepared backing; pin or baste layers together to hold.

Step 2. Hand- or machine-quilt as desired. When quilting is complete, trim batting and backing even with top; remove pins or basting.

Step 3. Join the previously cut binding strips on short ends to make one long strip. Fold the strip in half along length with wrong sides together; press.

Step 4. Sew binding to quilt edges, mitering corners and overlapping ends. Fold binding to the backside and stitch in place to finish. ◆

FARM ANIMAL BABY QUILT Placement Diagram 25" x 49"

HORSE
Cut 1 red scrap

SPOTS
Cut 1 each
blue scrap

×

2

3

4

1

Center

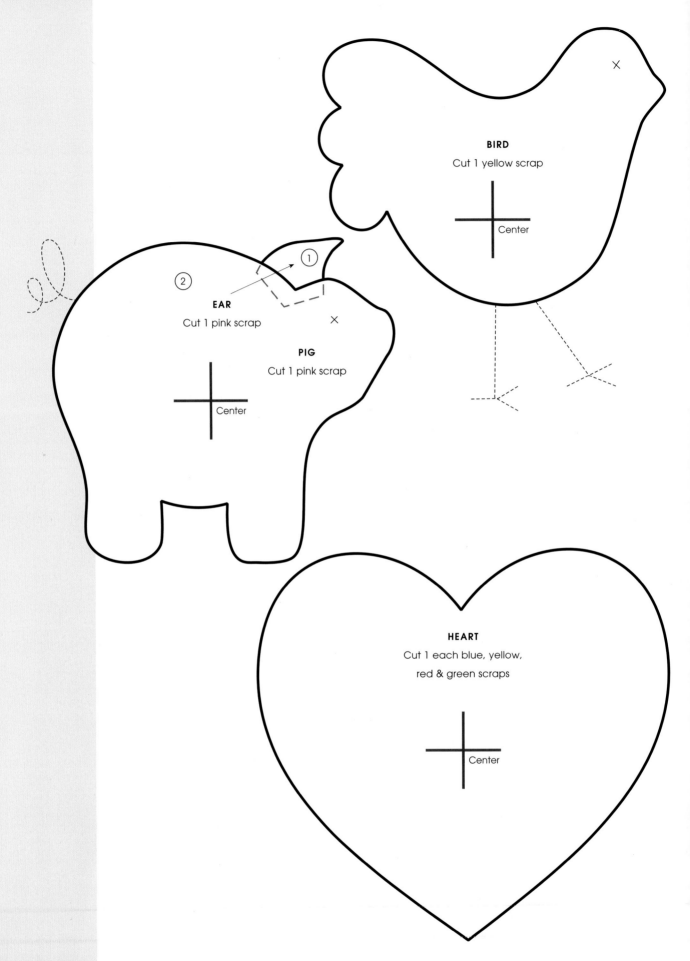

BIRD
Cut 1 yellow scrap

Center

EAR
Cut 1 pink scrap

PIG
Cut 1 pink scrap

Center

HEART
Cut 1 each blue, yellow,
red & green scraps

Center

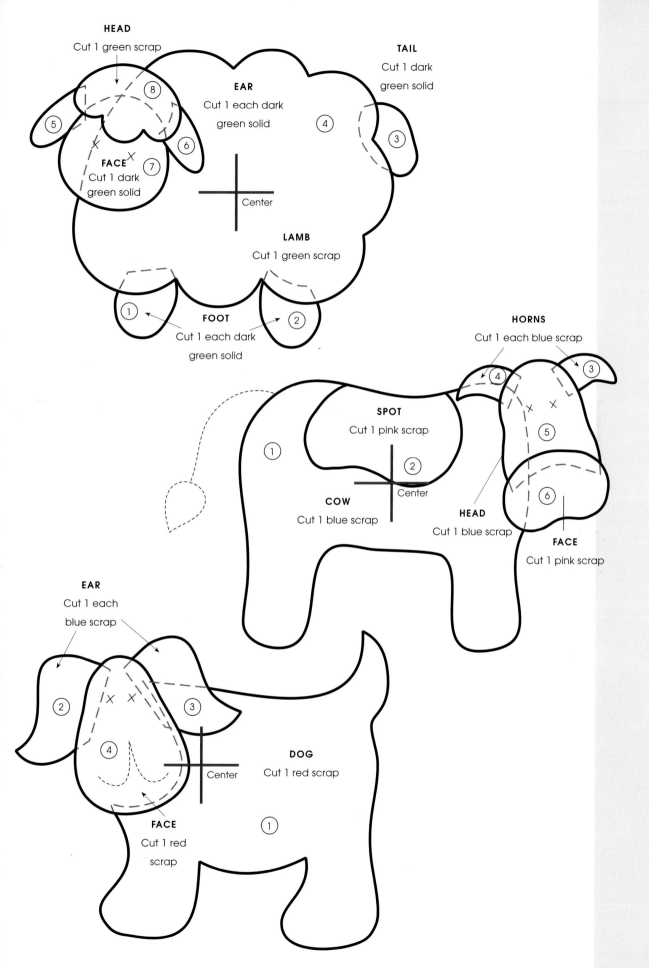

HEAD
Cut 1 green scrap

⑧

EAR
Cut 1 each dark
green solid

④

TAIL
Cut 1 dark
green solid

⑤

③

FACE
Cut 1 dark
green solid

⑦

⑥

Center

LAMB
Cut 1 green scrap

①

FOOT
Cut 1 each dark
green solid

②

HORNS
Cut 1 each blue scrap

④

③

SPOT
Cut 1 pink scrap

①

②

Center

⑤

COW
Cut 1 blue scrap

HEAD
Cut 1 blue scrap

⑥

FACE
Cut 1 pink scrap

EAR
Cut 1 each
blue scrap

②

③

④

Center

DOG
Cut 1 red scrap

FACE
Cut 1 red
scrap

①

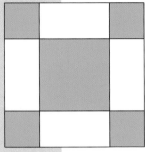

NINE-PATCH
6" x 6" Block

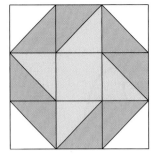

SPINNING STARS
6" x 6" Block

CHICK
6" x 6" Block

Here a Chick, There a Chick

DESIGN > JILL REBER

A juvenile print combines with bright scraps and an appliquéd chick in this cute child's quilt.

PROJECT SPECIFICATIONS
Skill Level: Intermediate
Quilt Size: 47" x 59"
Block Size: 6" x 6"
Number of Blocks: 35

MATERIALS
- Scraps gold and light blue fabrics
- 18 (4" x 10") rectangles different bright fabrics for pieced blocks
- ⅓ yard blue print for borders
- ⅓ yard yellow mottled for chicks
- ⅝ yard blue mottled for pieced blocks and binding
- 1¼ yards white solid for background
- 1⅞ yards juvenile print for borders
- Backing 53" x 65"
- Batting 53" x 65"
- Neutral color all-purpose thread
- Quilting thread
- Black and orange 6-strand embroidery floss for beaks and eyes
- Basic sewing tools and supplies

INSTRUCTIONS
Cutting
Step 1. Cut three 6½" by fabric width strips white solid; subcut into (17) 6½" A squares.

Step 2. Prepare template for chick; cut as directed on pattern, adding a ¼" seam allowance all around for hand appliqué.

Step 3. From each of the 18 bright fabric rectangles, cut one 3½" x 3½" B square and four 2" x 2" C squares.

Step 4. Cut four 3½" by fabric width strips white solid; subcut into (72) 2" D rectangles.

Step 5. Cut four 2" x 2" E squares white solid.

Step 6. Cut two 2" x 30½" F and two 2" x 42½" G strips blue print.

Step 7. Cut one 2⅞" by fabric width strip white solid; subcut strip into eight 2⅞" H squares. Draw a diagonal line on the wrong side of each H square.

Step 8. Cut eight 2⅞" x 2⅞" I squares each light blue scrap and blue mottled.

Step 9. Cut eight 2⅞" x 2⅞" J squares gold scrap; draw a diagonal line on the wrong side of each J square.

Step 10. Cut four 2½" x 2½" K squares gold scrap.

Step 11. Cut four 1½" x 6½" L strips and four 1½" x 7½" M strips juvenile print.

Step 12. Cut two 7½" x 33½" O strips across the width and two 7½" x 45½" N strips along the remaining length of the juvenile print.

Step 13. Cut six 2¼" by fabric width strips blue mottled for binding.

Completing Chick Blocks

Step 1. Fold and crease each A square to find the centers.

Step 2. Turn under edges of each chick shape ¼"; baste to hold.

Step 3. To complete one Chick block, center a fabric chick on an A square using creased lines and center mark on chick pattern as guides referring to **Figure 1**; baste to hold in place.

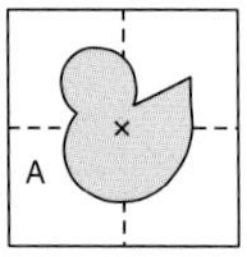

FIGURE 1
Center chick shape on A.

Step 4. Hand-stitch chick shapes in place using matching all-purpose thread.

Step 5. Transfer wing, eye, beak and feet details to stitched block using water-erasable marker or pencil.

Step 6. Satin-stitch beak using 3 strands orange embroidery floss. Straight-stitch feet, eye and wing details using 3 strands black embroidery floss to complete one block; repeat for 17 Chick blocks.

Completing Nine-Patch Blocks

Step 1. To complete one Nine-Patch block, select one color set of B and C pieces.

Step 2. Sew D to opposite sides of B; press seams toward B.

Step 3. Sew C to opposite ends of two D pieces; press seams toward C.

Step 4. Join the pieced units as shown in **Figure 2** to complete one Nine-Patch block; press seams toward B-D units. Repeat for 18 Nine-Patch blocks.

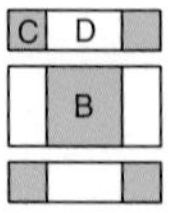

FIGURE 2 Join units to complete 1 Nine-Patch block.

Completing Spinning Stars Blocks

Step 1. Referring to **Figure 3**, place an H square right sides together with an I square; stitch ¼" on each side of the marked line. Cut apart on marked line; press open to complete two blue mottled H-I units. Repeat to make eight each light blue scrap and blue mottled H-I units.

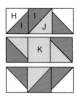

FIGURE 3 Complete an H-I unit as shown.

Step 2. Repeat Step 1 with remaining I squares and J to complete eight each light blue scrap and blue mottled I-J units.

Step 3. Arrange the H-I and I-J units in rows with K as shown in **Figure 4**; join units in rows. Press seams in top and bottom rows toward H-I units and toward K in the center row; stitch to complete one Spinning Star block; repeat for four blocks (two each light blue scrap and blue mottled).

FIGURE 4 Arrange and join pieced units with K to complete 1 Spinning Star block.

Completing the Top

Step 1. Join three Nine-Patch blocks and two Chick blocks to make a row referring to **Figure 5**; press seams toward Chick blocks. Repeat for four rows.

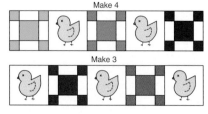

FIGURE 5 Join blocks to make rows.

Step 2. Join three Chick blocks with two Nine-Patch blocks to make a row, again referring to Figure 5; press seams toward Chick blocks. Repeat for three rows.

Step 3. Join the rows referring to the Placement Diagram for positioning; press seams in one direction.

Step 4. Sew a G strip to opposite long sides; press seams toward G. Sew an E square to each end of each F strip; press seams toward F. Sew an E-F strip to the top and bottom of the pieced center; press seams toward strips.

Step 5. Sew L to the bottom and M to one side of each Spinning Star block as shown in **Figure 6**; press seams toward L and M.

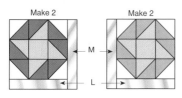

FIGURE 6 Sew L to the bottom and M to 1 side of each spinning star block.

Step 6. Sew an N strip to opposite long sides of the pieced center; press seams toward N.

Step 7. Sew a bordered Spinning Star block to each end of each O strip as shown in **Figure 7**; press seams toward O. Sew a block/O strip to the top and bottom of the pieced center to complete the top; press seams toward block/O strips.

FIGURE 7 Sew a bordered Spinning Star block to each end of each O strip.

Finishing the Quilt

Step 1. Sandwich the batting between the completed top and prepared backing; pin or baste layers together to hold.

Step 2. Hand- or machine-quilt as desired. When quilting is complete, trim batting and backing even with top; remove pins or basting.

Step 3. Join the previously cut binding strips on short ends to make one long strip. Fold the strip in half along length with wrong sides together; press.

Step 4. Sew binding to quilt edges, mitering corners and overlapping ends. Fold binding to the backside and stitch in place. ◆

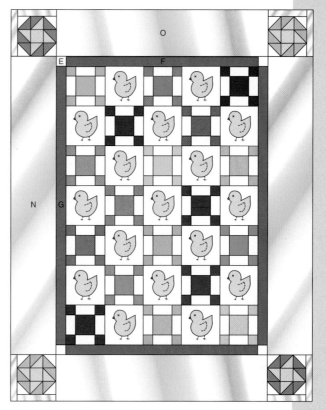

HERE A CHICK, THERE A CHICK Placement Diagram 47" x 59"

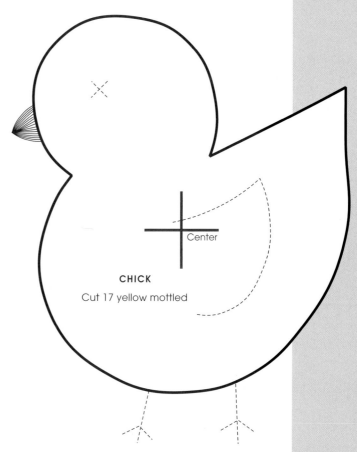

CHICK
Cut 17 yellow mottled

Add a ¼" seam allowance all around when cutting for hand appliqué.

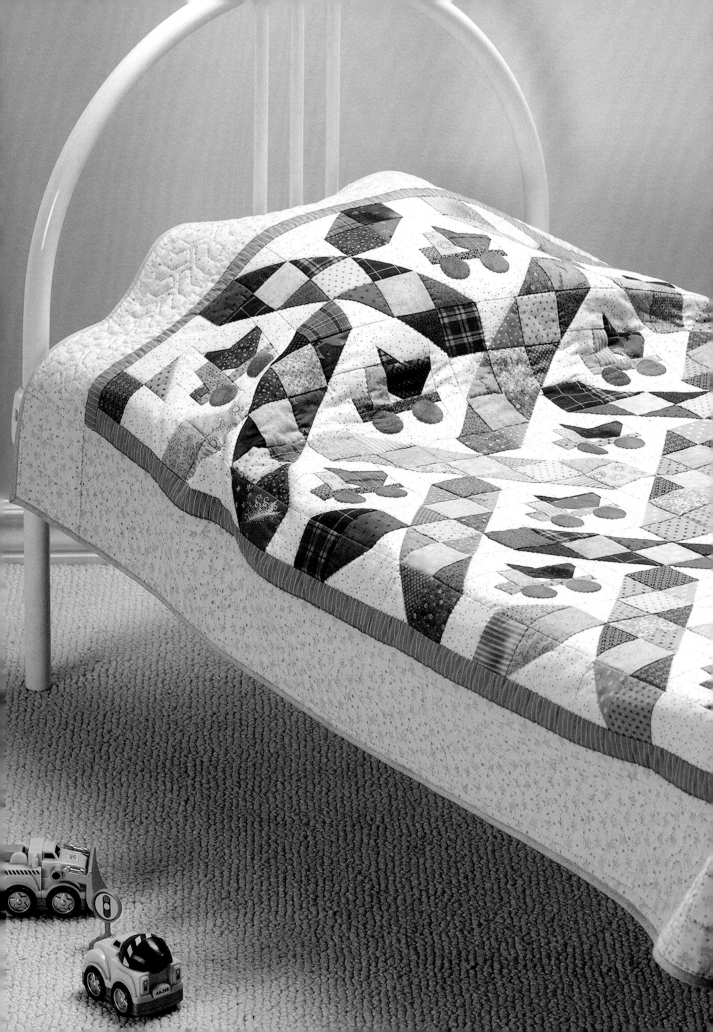

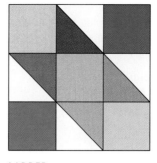

LADDER
6" x 6" Block

TRUCK
6" x 6" Block

Road Crew Rally

DESIGN > JODI WARNER

Any little boy would love a quilt with this

paper-pieced dump truck design.

PROJECT SPECIFICATIONS
Skill Level: Advanced
Quilt Size: 46" x 58"
Block Size: 6" x 6"
Number of Blocks: 35

MATERIALS
- Scraps assorted teal, blue, violet, pink and yellow fabrics
- Scraps assorted tan fabrics
- Scrap dark tan for wheels
- ¼ yard light blue stripe for narrow border
- ½ yard binding fabric
- 1 yard yellow print for outer border
- 1¼ yards cream star for background
- Backing 52" x 64"
- Batting 52" x 64"
- Neutral color all-purpose thread
- Quilting thread
- Clear nylon monofilament
- Card stock
- Basic sewing tools and supplies

INSTRUCTIONS
Making Truck Blocks
Step 1. Prepare 18 copies of the truck foundation pattern. Complete paper-pieced blocks adding pieces in numerical order using scraps in colors suggested on pattern. For each pair of front and back sections that create one block, use one scrap from each of the five color fabrics.

Step 2. Trim excess fabrics and paper foundation on outer solid lines.

Step 3. Transfer wheel circle positions to fabric fronts using temporary marker. Remove paper foundation.

Step 4. Join front and back sections at vertical seam; press seam toward truck back to complete one truck unit. Repeat for 18 truck units.

Step 5. Cut 3¼" x 3¼" scrap squares as follows: six each teal, blue, violet and nine each pink and yellow. Cut each square in half on one diagonal to make A triangles; organize A Triangles by color.

Step 6. Arrange A pieces at truck unit corners referring to **Figure 1**. *Note: It is important to place the correct color on each corner of each block to create quilt design.*

FIGURE 1 Add A triangles to truck unit corners to make 3 blocks of each combination.

Step 7. Center a triangle along corner cut edge (triangle edge is cut larger than necessary to allow for trimming to size), stitch and press seam toward block as shown in **Figure 2**. Repeat on all four corners of a truck unit and trim excess A corner edges square with block as shown in **Figure 3** to make a 6½" x 6½" block; repeat to make 18 Truck blocks.

FIGURE 2 Stitch and press seam toward A.

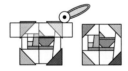

FIGURE 3 Trim excess A edges square with block.

Step 8. Photocopy card-stock circles as directed on pattern; cut out circles for truck wheels.

Step 9. Cut 36 dark tan fabric circles, using card-stock circles and adding ¼" all around for seam allowance. Hand-baste a gathering stitch all around fabric circle within the ¼" seam allowance. Place card-stock circle within basting against the wrong side of the fabric circle; pull to gather around circle and backstitch to secure as shown in **Figure 4**. Do not remove card-stock circle; repeat with all circles.

FIGURE 4 Gather around card-stock circle and backstitch.

Step 10. Pin two prepared circles on a Truck block; referring to foundation pattern for positioning.

Step 11. Attach folded edge to block using clear nylon monofilament and invisible machine swing stitch so that straight stitches fall just beyond circle edge through block only and swing zigzag catches threads at circle folded edge. Press with medium-warm iron.

Step 12. Trim away excess fabric behind wheel circles, leaving a ¼" seam allowance; pop the card-stock circle out through opening.

Completing Ladder Blocks

Step 1. Cut 2⅞" x 2⅞" scrap B squares as follows: seven teal, eight each blue and violet, 10 pink and 11 yellow. Cut (44) 2⅞" x 2⅞" cream star squares for C.

Step 2. Draw a diagonal line from corner to corner on the wrong side of each C square.

Step 3. Place C right sides together with a scrap B; stitch ¼" on both sides of the marked line. Cut apart on the marked line; press open with seam toward B to yield two B-C units as shown in **Figure 5**. Repeat with all B and C squares.

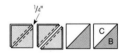

FIGURE 5 Stitch ¼" on each side of line; cut apart to yield 2 B-C units.

Step 4. Cut (51) 2½" x 2½" tan scrap D squares.

Step 5. Cut 2½" x 2½" scrap E squares as follows: four teal, six each blue and violet, eight pink and 10 yellow.

Step 6. Arrange B-C units with D and E squares in rows as shown in **Figure 6**.

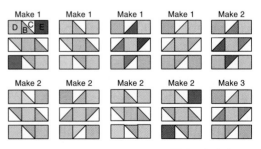

FIGURE 6 Join B-C units with D and E squares in rows to complete Ladder blocks.

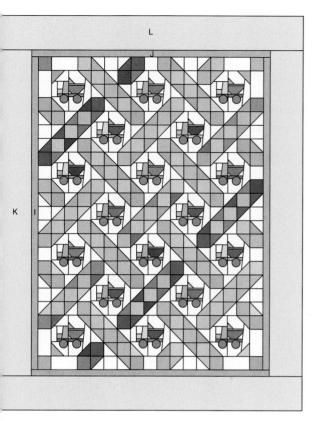

ROAD CRE RALL Y Placement Diagram 46" 58"

side and top and bottom borders by alternating remaining B-C units, F and H squares and G rectangles as shown in **Figure 7**; press seams toward color side of seams.

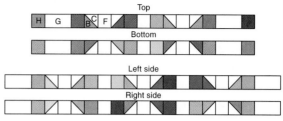

FIGURE 7 Join squares and rectangles with B-C units to make borders.

Step 5. Sew longer strips to opposite sides and shorter strips to the top and bottom of the pieced center; press seams toward strips. *Note: The Ladder blocks appear to extend into the borders so that color placement is important; refer to the Placement Diagram and color photo for positioning of strips.*

Step 6. Cut (and piece) two 1½" x 46½" I strips and two 1½" x 36½" J strips light blue stripe. Sew I to opposite long sides and J to the top and bottom of the pieced center; press seams toward strips.

Step 7. Cut and piece two 5½" x 48½" K strips and two 5½" x 46½" L strips yellow print. Sew K to opposite long sides and L to the top and bottom of the pieced center; press seams toward strips.

Step 7. Join the units and squares in rows; join the rows to complete one block; repeat for 17 blocks. Press seams toward D and E squares. Set aside remaining B-C units for borders.

Completing the Top

Step 1. Arrange the Truck and Ladder blocks referring to the Placement Diagram for positioning; join three Truck blocks with two Ladder blocks to make a row. Repeat for four rows. Press seams toward Ladder blocks. *Note: It may be helpful to arrange an overall layout on the floor or other large working surface to maintain truck and ladder order as blocks are joined. This will more clearly show how colors from adjoining blocks complete the color ladder shapes along the diagonal of the quilt top.*

Step 2. Join three Ladder blocks with two Truck blocks to make a row; repeat for three rows. Press seams toward Ladder blocks.

Step 3. Cut 16 F squares 2½" x 2½" and eight G rectangles 2½" x 4½" cream star. Cut 2½" x 2½" scrap H squares as follows: four each teal, blue and violet and six each pink and yellow.

Step 4. Arrange and assemble left and right

Finishing the Quilt

Step 1. Sandwich the batting between the completed top and prepared backing; pin or baste layers together to hold.

Step 2. Hand- or machine-quilt as desired. When quilting is complete, trim batting and backing even with top; remove pins or basting. *Note: A quilting design is given for outside borders. The border corners are quilted in a mock Nine-Patch design.*

Step 3. Cut six strips binding fabric 2¼" by fabric width.

Join the strips on short ends to make one long strip. Fold the strip in half along length with wrong sides together; press.

Step 4. Sew binding to quilt edges, mitering corners and overlapping ends. Fold binding to the backside and stitch in place. ◆

Border seam

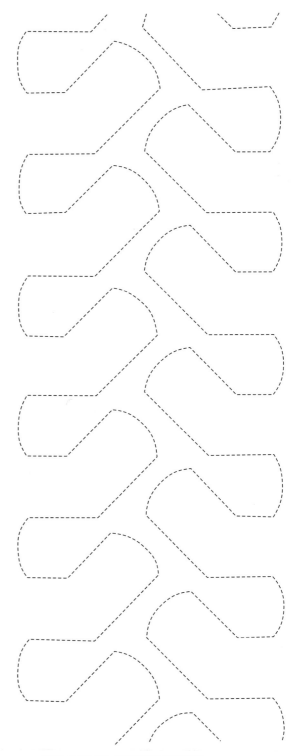

TRUCK TREAD QUILTING DESIGN

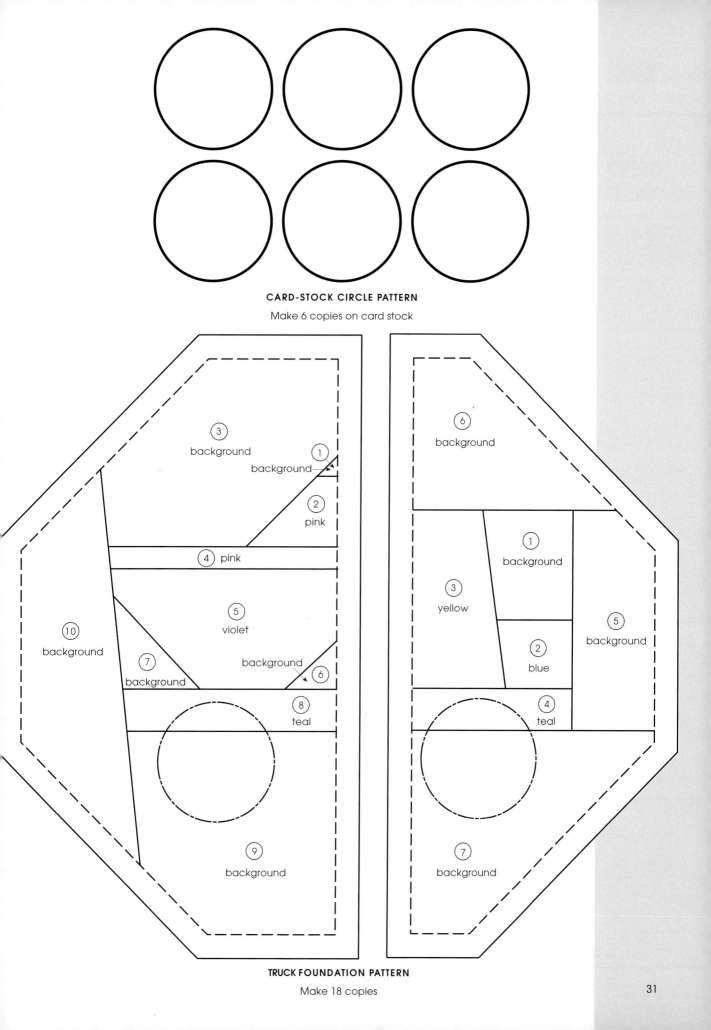

CARD-STOCK CIRCLE PATTERN

Make 6 copies on card stock

3 background

1 background

2 pink

4 pink

5 violet

10 background

7 background

background

6

8 teal

9 background

6 background

1 background

3 yellow

2 blue

5 background

4 teal

7 background

TRUCK FOUNDATION PATTERN

Make 18 copies

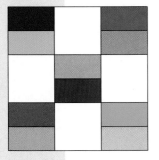

DOT NINE-PATCH
6" x 6" Block

CROSSED DOTS
6" x 6" Block

Polka-Dot Party

DESIGN > CONNIE KAUFFMAN

Bright polka-dots make this quilt a cheerful addition to any room.

PROJECT SPECIFICATIONS

Skill Level: Beginner
Quilt Size: 42" x 42"
Block Size: 6" x 6"
Number of Blocks: 25

MATERIALS

- 1 fat quarter each 6 or more polka-dot fabrics
- 1 fat quarter each 5 bright fabrics
- ³⁄₈ yard white tonal
- ½ yard white background with dots (white dot)
- ½ yard green background with dots (green dot)
- 1 yard purple background with dots (purple dot)
- Backing 48" x 48"
- Batting 48" x 48"
- Neutral color all-purpose thread
- Quilting thread
- Basic tools and supplies

INSTRUCTIONS

Cutting

Step 1. Cut four 2½" by fabric width strips white tonal; subcut strips into (52) 2½" A squares.

Step 2. Cut (65) 1½" x 2½" B rectangles from the polka-dot fabrics. Repeat to cut 65 B rectangles from the five bright fabrics.

Step 3. Cut six 7¼" x 7¼" squares each purple dot (C) and white dot (D); cut each square in half on both diagonals to make 24 each C and D triangles.

Step 4. Cut two 3½" x 30½" E strips and two 3½" x 36½" F strips green dot.

Step 5. Cut approximately 20 G strips each polka-dot and bright fabrics 2" x 7"–2" x 11" for pieced outside borders.

Step 6. Cut five 2¼" by fabric width strips purple dot for binding.

Piecing Blocks

Step 1. Join one each polka-dot and bright B

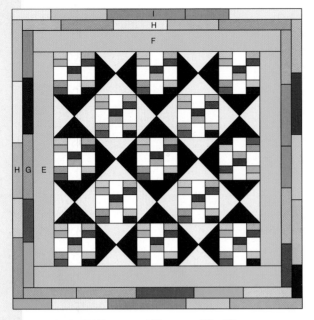

POLKA-DOT PARTY Placement Diagram 42" x 42"

rectangles on the 2½" sides to make a B unit; repeat for 65 B units.

Step 2. To complete one Dot Nine-Patch block, join two B units with A to make a row as shown in **Figure 1**; repeat for two rows. Press seams toward B units.

Step 3. Join one B unit with two A squares to make a row, again referring to **Figure 1**; press seams toward B unit.

Make 1

Make 2

FIGURE 1 Join A squares and B units to make rows as shown.

FIGURE 2 Join rows to complete 1 block.

Step 4. Join the rows to complete one Dot Nine-Patch block as shown in **Figure 2**; press seams in one direction. Repeat for 13 blocks.

Step 5. To piece one Crossed Dots block, sew C to D as shown in **Figure 3**; repeat for two C-D units. Press seams toward C.

FIGURE 3 Sew C to D.

FIGURE 4 Join units to complete 1 block.

Step 6. Join two C-D units to complete one Crossed Dots block as shown in **Figure 4**; press seams in one direction. Repeat for 12 blocks.

Completing the Top

Step 1. Join three Dot Nine-Patch blocks with two Crossed Dots blocks to make a row referring to **Figure 5**; press seams toward Crossed Dots blocks. Repeat for three rows.

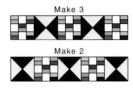

FIGURE 5 Join blocks to make rows.

Step 2. Join three Crossed Dots blocks with two Dot Nine-Patch blocks to make a row, again referring to **Figure 5**; press seams toward Crossed Dots blocks. Repeat for two rows.

Step 3. Join the rows referring to the Placement Diagram; press seams in one direction.

Step 4. Sew E strips to opposite sides and F strips to the top and bottom of the pieced center; press seams toward strips.

Step 5. Join the G strips on short ends to make one long strip, alternating polka-dot and bright strips; press seams in one direction.

Step 6. Cut two strips each 36½" (G), 42½" (I) and four strips 39½" (H).

Step 7. Sew G to opposite sides and H to the top and bottom of the pieced center; press seams toward E and F. Sew H to opposite sides and I to the top and bottom of the pieced center; press seams toward H and I.

Finishing the Quilt

Step 1. Sandwich the batting between the completed top and prepared backing piece; pin or baste to hold.

Step 2. Hand- or machine-quilt as desired.

Step 3. Trim batting and backing even with the quilted top.

Step 4. Join the binding strips on short ends with a diagonal seam to make a long strip; press seams toward one side.

Step 5. Press the strip in half along length with wrong sides together to complete the binding strip. Bind edges of quilt to finish. ◆

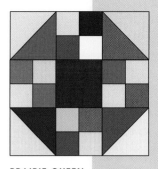

PRAIRIE QUEEN
15" x 15"

Scrappy Prairie Queen

DESIGN > SANDRA L. HATCH

Select a variety of light and dark scraps

to make this quick bed-size quilt.

PROJECT SPECIFICATIONS

Skill Level: Beginner
Quilt Size: 85" x 100"
Block Size: 15" x 15"
Number of Blocks: 20

MATERIALS

- ¾ yard cream tonal
- 2¾ yards total light scraps
- 2¾ yards dark floral print
- 3½ yards total dark scraps
- Backing 91" x 106"
- Batting 91" x 106"
- Neutral color all-purpose thread
- Quilting thread
- Basic sewing tools and supplies

INSTRUCTIONS
Cutting
Step 1. Cut 40 squares each light and dark scraps 5⅞" x 5⅞" for A. ***Note:*** *Six 5⅞" by fabric width strips to equal 1 yard each light and dark are needed if cutting strips from scrap fabric.*

Step 2. Cut and piece 3"-wide strips from light and dark scraps to equal (18) 3" x 42" strips each for B unit. ***Note:*** *If using unpieced scrap strips, only 16 strips (or 1½ yards total) are needed.*

Step 3. Cut 24 squares dark scraps 5½" x 5½" for C.

Step 4. Cut seven 3" by fabric width strips cream tonal for D and E.

Step 5. Cut nine 8" by fabric width strips dark floral print for F.

Step 6. Cut ten 2¼" by fabric width strips dark floral print for binding.

Piecing the Blocks
Step 1. Draw a diagonal line from corner to corner on the wrong side of each light A square.

Step 2. Place a marked A square right sides together with a dark A square; stitch ¼" on each side of the marked line as shown in **Figure 1**. Repeat for all A squares.

FIGURE 1 Stitch ¼" on each side of the marked line.

Step 3. Cut a stitched A unit on the marked line; press seams toward the dark A pieces to complete two A units as shown in **Figure 2**. Repeat for all A units.

Step 4. Sew a light B strip to a dark B strip with right sides together along length; press seams toward dark B. Repeat for 18 strip sets.

FIGURE 2 Cut a stitched A unit on the marked line to make 2 A units.

Step 5. Subcut strip sets into (214) 3" B units as shown in **Figure 3**; set aside 54 units for borders.

FIGURE 3 Subcut strip sets into 3" B units.

FIGURE 4 Join 2 A units with a B unit.

Step 6. To piece one block, join two A units with a B unit as shown in **Figure 4**; press seams open. Repeat for two A-B rows.

Step 7. Join two B units with C referring to **Figure 5**; press seams toward C.

FIGURE 5 Join 2 B units with C.

FIGURE 6 Join rows to complete 1 block.

Step 8. Join the A-B rows with the B-C row to complete one block as shown in **Figure 6**; press seams open. Repeat for 20 blocks.

Completing the Top

Step 1. Arrange the blocks in five rows of four blocks each. When satisfied with the arrangement, join blocks in rows; press seams open. Join the rows to complete the pieced center; press seams open.

Step 2. Join 15 B units on short ends to make a border strip as shown in **Figure 7**; repeat for two strips. Repeat with 12 B units to complete two strips.

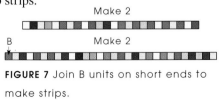

Make 2

Make 2

FIGURE 7 Join B units on short ends to make strips.

Step 3. Join the D and E strips on the short ends to complete one long strip; press seams open. Cut

SCRAPPY PRAIRIE QUEEN Placement Diagram 85" x 100"

two 75½" D and two 60½" E strips from the strip.

Step 4. Sew a D strip to each 15-unit B strip and an E strip to each 12-unit B strip; press seams toward D and E. Sew a D strip to opposite sides of the pieced center with B units on the outside edge referring to the Placement Diagram.

Step 5. Sew a C square to each end of each B-E strip; press seams away from C. Sew a strip to the top and bottom of the pieced center with B units on the outside edge referring to the Placement Diagram.

Step 6. Join the F strips on the short ends to make one long strip; press seams open. Cut four 85½" F strips from the strip.

Step 7. Sew an F strip to opposite long sides and to the top and bottom of the pieced center to complete the top; press seams toward F.

Finishing the Quilt

Step 1. Sandwich the batting between the completed top and prepared backing; pin or baste layers together to hold.

Step 2. Hand- or machine-quilt as desired. When quilting is complete, trim batting and backing even with top; remove pins or basting.

Step 3. Join the previously cut binding strips on short ends to make one long strip. Fold the strip in half along length with wrong sides together; press.

Step 4. Sew binding to quilt edges, mitering corners and overlapping ends. Fold binding to the backside and stitch in place to finish. ◆

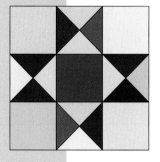

STAR
9" x 9" Block

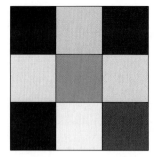

NINE-PATCH
9" x 9" Block

Star-Spangled
Scrap Quilt

DESIGN > PEARL LOUISE KRUSH

Scraps in red, cream and blue combine in Star and Nine-

Patch blocks to give this quilt a patriotic flare.

PROJECT SPECIFICATIONS
Skill Level: Beginner
Quilt Size: 58" x 76"
Block Size: 9" x 9"
Number of Blocks: 35

MATERIALS
- Blue scraps to total ½ yard
- Red scraps to total 1¼ yards
- Cream scraps to total 2 yards
- 1 yard red print
- 1¼ yards dark blue print
- Backing 64" x 82"
- Batting 64" x 82"
- Neutral color all-purpose thread
- Quilting thread
- Basic tools and supplies

INSTRUCTIONS
Cutting
Step 1. Cut (35) 3½" x 3½" squares blue scraps for A.

Step 2. Cut (68) 3½" x 3½" squares red scraps for B.

Step 3. Cut (36) 4¼" x 4¼" squares each red (C) and cream (E) scraps; cut each square on both diagonals to make 144 each C and E triangles.

Step 4. Cut (140) 3½" x 3½" squares cream scraps for D.

Step 5. Cut six 2½" by fabric width strips dark blue print for F and G borders.

Step 6. Cut four 5" x 5" J squares dark blue print.

Step 7. Cut six 5" by fabric width strips red print for H and I borders.

Step 8. Cut seven 2¼" by fabric width strips dark blue print for binding.

Piecing Star Blocks
Step 1. To piece one Star block, sew C to E as shown in **Figure 1**; press seam toward C. Repeat for two units. Join units to complete a C-E unit, again referring to **Figure 1**; repeat for four C-E units.

FIGURE 1

Complete
C-E units as
shown.

Step 2. Join a C-E unit with two D squares to make a row as shown in **Figure 2**; repeat for two rows. Press seams toward D.

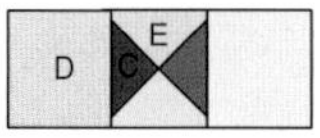

FIGURE 2 Join a C-E unit with 2 D squares to make a row.

Step 3. Join two C-E units with A to make a row as shown in **Figure 3**; press seams toward A.

FIGURE 3 Join 2 C-E units with A to make a row.

Step 4. Join the rows to complete a Star block as shown in **Figure 4**; press seams in one direction. Repeat for 18 Star blocks.

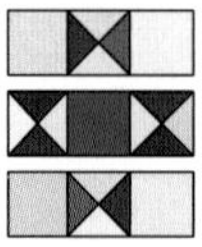

FIGURE 4 Join the rows to complete a Star block.

Piecing Nine-Patch Blocks
Step 1. Join two B squares with one D square to make a row as shown in **Figure 5**; repeat for two rows. Press seams toward B.

FIGURE 5 Join 2 B squares with 1 D square to make a row.

Step 2. Join two D squares with one A square to make a row as shown in **Figure 6**; press seams toward A.

FIGURE 6 Join 2 D squares with 1 A square to make a row.

Step 3. Join the rows to complete a Nine-Patch block as shown in **Figure 7**; press seams in one direction. Repeat for 17 Nine-Patch blocks.

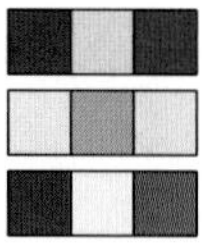

FIGURE 7 Join the rows to complete a Nine-Patch block.

Completing the Quilt

Step 1. Join three Star blocks with two Nine-Patch blocks to make a row referring to **Figure 8**; repeat for four rows. Press seams toward Nine-Patch blocks.

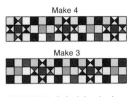

FIGURE 8 Join blocks to make rows.

Step 2. Join three Nine-Patch blocks with two Star blocks to make a row, again referring to **Figure 8**; repeat for three rows. Press seams toward Nine-Patch blocks.

Step 3. Join the rows referring to the Placement Diagram to complete the pieced center; press seams in one direction.

Step 4. Join the F/G strips on short ends to make one long strip; press seams in one direction. Cut the F/G strip into two 63½" F strips and two 49½" G strips. Sew an F strip to opposite long sides and a G strip to the top and bottom of the pieced center; press seams toward F and G.

Step 5. Join the H/I strips on short ends to make one long strip; press seams in one direction. Cut the H/I strip into two 67½" H strips and two 49½" I strips. Sew an H strip to opposite sides of the pieced center; press seams toward H.

Step 6. Sew a J square to each end of each I strip; press seams toward I. Sew an I-J strip to the top and bottom of the pieced center; press seams toward I-J strips.

STAR-SPANGLED SCRAP QUILT Placement Diagram 58" x 76"

Finishing the Quilt

Step 1. Sandwich the batting between the completed top and prepared backing piece; pin or baste to hold.

Step 2. Hand- or machine-quilt as desired.

Step 3. Trim batting and backing even with the quilted top.

Step 4. Join the binding strips on short ends with a diagonal seam to make a long strip; press seams toward one side.

Step 5. Press the strip in half along length with wrong sides together to complete the binding strip. Bind edges of quilt to finish. ◆

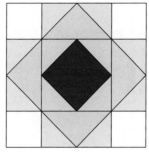

SQUARE-IN-A-SQUARE
12" x 12" Block

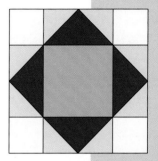

FRAMED SQUARE
12" x 12" Block

Diamonds on Parade

DESIGN > JUDITH SANDSTROM

Blend lots of blue fabrics in this quilt made with two

different pieced blocks.

PROJECT SPECIFICATIONS

Skill Level: Beginner
Quilt Size: 78" x 90"
Block Size: 12" x 12"
Number of Blocks: 30

MATERIALS

- ¼ yard each 10 blue/tan prints
- ⅔ yard light blue print for binding
- 1⅛ yards cream tonal
- 1¼ yards tan tonal
- 1½ yards light blue tonal
- 2 yards dark blue tonal
- Backing 84" x 96"
- Batting 84" x 96"
- Neutral color all-purpose thread
- Quilting thread
- Basic sewing tools and supplies

INSTRUCTIONS

Cutting

Step 1. Cut ten 3½" by fabric width strips cream tonal; subcut into (120) 3½" B squares.

Step 2. Cut the following fabric width strips from dark blue tonal: three 7¼"—subcut into (15) 7¼" C squares and cut each C square in half on both diagonals to make 60 C triangles; two 4¾"—subcut into (15) 4¾" E squares; and eight 3½" for H and I borders. Cut four 3½" x 6½" J rectangles dark blue tonal.

Step 3. Cut twelve 3⅞" by fabric width strips light blue tonal; subcut strips into (120) 3⅞" D squares. Cut each square on one diagonal to make 240 D triangles.

Step 4. Cut the following fabric width strips tan tonal; three 7¼"—subcut strips into (15) 7¼" F squares and cut each square on both diagonals to make (60) F triangles; and three 3⅞"—subcut into (30) 3⅞" G squares and cut each square on one diagonal to make (60) G triangles. Cut four 6½" x 6½" K squares tan tonal.

Step 5. Cut one 6½" by fabric width strip from each of the 10 prints; subcut strips into (59) 6½" A squares.

Step 6. Cut nine 2¼" by fabric width strips light blue print for binding.

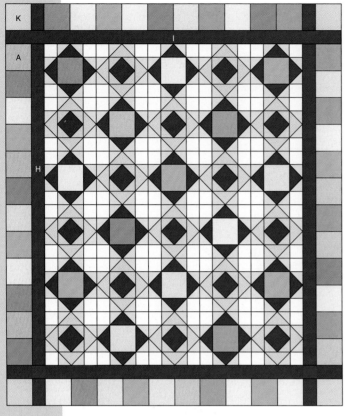

Piecing Square-in-a-Square Blocks

Step 1. To piece one Square-in-a-Square block, sew G to each side of E as shown in **Figure 1**; press seams toward G.

FIGURE 1 Sew G to
each side of E.

Step 2. Sew D to two sides of F as shown in **Figure 2**; press seams toward D. Repeat for four D-F units.

FIGURE 2 Sew D to 2
sides of F.

Step 3. Sew a D-F unit to opposite sides of the E-G unit as shown in **Figure 3**; press seams toward D-F.

FIGURE 3 Sew a D-F unit to
opposite sides of the E-G unit.

Step 4. Sew a B square to opposite ends of the remaining D-F units as shown in **Figure 4**; press seams away from B.

FIGURE 4 Sew a B square
to opposite ends of the
remaining D-F units.

Step 5. Sew a B-D-F unit to opposite sides of the E-G-D-F unit to complete one Square-in-a-Square block as shown in **Figure 5**; press seams toward B-D-F units. Repeat to make 15 blocks.

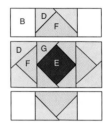

FIGURE 5 Sew 2 B-D-F units to
the E-G-D-F unit to complete 1
Square-in-a-Square block.

Piecing Framed Square Blocks

Step 1. To piece one Framed Square block, sew D to two sides of C as in **Figure 2** for D and F; press seams toward D. Repeat for four C-D units.
Step 2. Sew a C-D unit to opposite sides of A as shown in **Figure 6**; press seams toward A.

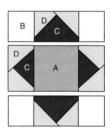

FIGURE 6 Sew 2 B-C-D units to
the A-C-D unit to complete 1
Framed Square block.

Step 3. Sew a B square to each end of the remaining C-D units as in **Figure 4** for D-F units; press seams toward B.
Step 4. Sew a B-C-D unit to opposite sides of the A-C-D unit to complete one Framed Square block as shown in **Figure 6**; press seams toward A-C-D units. Repeat for 15 blocks.

Completing the Pieced Top

Step 1. Join three Framed Square blocks with two Square-in-a-Square blocks to make a row referring to **Figure 7**; press seams toward Square-in-a-Square blocks. Repeat for three rows.

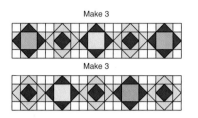

FIGURE 7 Join blocks to make rows.

Step 2. Join three Square-in-a-Square blocks with two Framed Square blocks to make a row, again referring to **Figure 7**; press seams toward Square-in-a-Square blocks. Repeat for three rows.

Step 3. Join the rows to complete the pieced center; press seams in one direction.

Step 4. Join the 3½"-wide dark blue tonal strips on short ends to make one long strip. Cut strip into two 72½" H strips and two 78½" I strips.

Step 5. Join 12 A squares to make a long strip; press seams in one direction. Repeat for two strips.

Step 6. Sew an A strip to H as shown in **Figure 8**; press seams toward H. Repeat for two A-H strips.

FIGURE 8 Sew an A strip to H.

Step 7. Sew an A-H strip to opposite sides of the pieced center with H on the inside; press seams toward H.

Step 8. Join 10 A squares to make a long strip; press seams in one direction. Sew J and then K to each end of each strip as shown in **Figure 9**; press seams toward J. Repeat for two A-J-K strips.

FIGURE 9 Sew J and then K to each end of the strip.

Step 9. Sew an A-J-K strip to I; press seam toward I. Repeat for two A-J-K-I strips. Sew a strip to the top and bottom to complete the pieced top; press seams toward strips.

Finishing the Quilt

Step 1. Sandwich the batting between the completed top and prepared backing; pin or baste layers together to hold.

Step 2. Hand- or machine-quilt as desired. When quilting is complete, trim batting and backing even with top; remove pins or basting.

Step 3. Join the previously cut binding strips on short ends to make one long strip. Fold the strip in half along length with wrong sides together; press.

Step 4. Sew binding to quilt edges, mitering corners and overlapping ends. Fold binding to the backside and stitch in place to finish. ◆

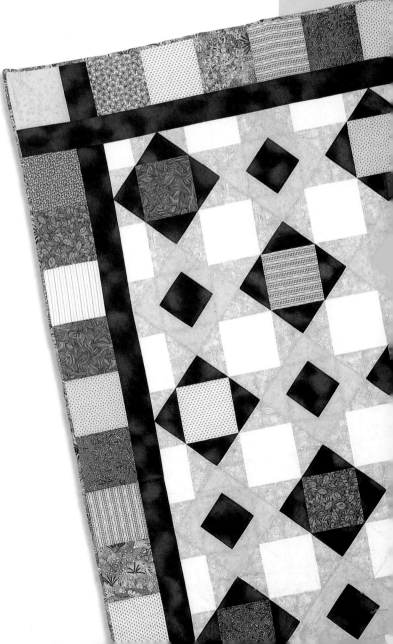

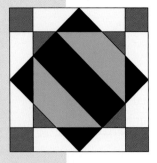

RANDOM COLORS
12" 12" Block

Random
Colors

DESIGN > CONNIE RAND

Bright novelty prints are tied together with black solid in this colorful quilt.

PROJECT SPECIFICATIONS
Skill Level: Beginner
Quilt Size: 64" x 76"
Block Size: 12" x 12"
Number of Blocks: 20

MATERIALS
- ½ yard binding fabric
- ¾ yard total bright novelty scraps
- ¾ yard total dark scraps
- 1¼ yards total light scraps
- 1⅜ yards bright multicolor print
- 1½ yards black solid
- Backing 70" x 82"
- Batting 70" x 82"
- Neutral color all-purpose thread
- Quilting thread
- Basic sewing tools and supplies

INSTRUCTIONS
Note: The sample uses one light print, one dark print and one novelty print for each block. For an extra scrappy quilt, try using a different print in every piece.

Making Blocks
Step 1. Cut (40) 2⅞" x 2⅞" squares for E and (80) 2½" x 2½" squares for F from dark scraps. Cut E squares in half on one diagonal to make 80 E triangles.

Step 2. Prepare templates for A–D pieces using patterns given; cut as directed on each piece for one block. Repeat for 20 blocks.

Step 3. Sew a C triangle to each angled edge of B as shown in **Figure 1**; press seams toward C.

FIGURE 1 Sew C to each angled edge of B.

FIGURE 2 Sew a B-C unit to each side of A.

Step 4. Sew a B-C unit to each side of A as shown in **Figure 2**; press seams toward A.

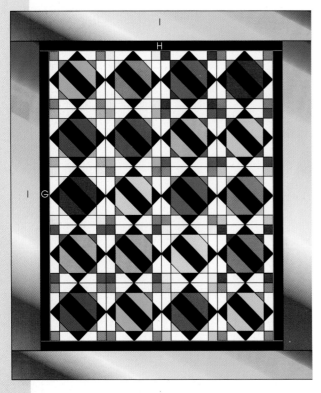

RANDOM COLORS Placement Diagram 64" 76"

Completing the Top

Step 1. Join blocks in five rows of four blocks each as shown in **Figure 5**; press seams in adjacent rows in opposite directions.

Make R

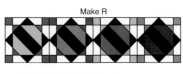

FIGURE 5 Join blocks in rows.

Step 2. Join rows to complete quilt center; press seams in one direction.

Step 3. Cut and piece two 2½" x 60½" G strips and two 2½" x 52½" H strips black solid.

Step 4. Sew G to opposite sides and H to the top and bottom of the pieced center; press seams toward strips.

Step 5. Cut and piece four 6½" x 64½" bright multicolor print I strips. Sew I to opposite sides and top and bottom of the pieced center to complete the quilt top; press seams toward I strips.

Finishing the Quilt

Step 1. Prepare quilt top for quilting and quilt referring to the General Instructions.

Step 2. When quilting is complete, trim batting and backing edges even with the quilted top.

Step 3. Cut seven 2¼" by fabric width strips binding fabric. Join strips on short ends to make one long strip. Fold the strip in half along length with wrong sides together; press.

Step 4. Sew binding to quilt edges, mitering corners and overlapping ends. Fold binding to the backside and stitch in place to finish. ◆

Step 5. Sew D to F and DR to E as shown in Figure 3; press seams toward E and F. Join the units again referring to **Figure 3**.

FIGURE 3 Sew D to F and
DR to E; join units as shown.

Step 6. Sew a D-E-F unit to each side of the A-B-C unit to complete one block as shown in **Figure 4**; press seams toward D-E-F units. Repeat for 20 blocks.

FIGURE 4 Join units to
complete the block as shown.

C
Cut 4 black solid

D
Cut 8 light scrap
(reverse half for DR)

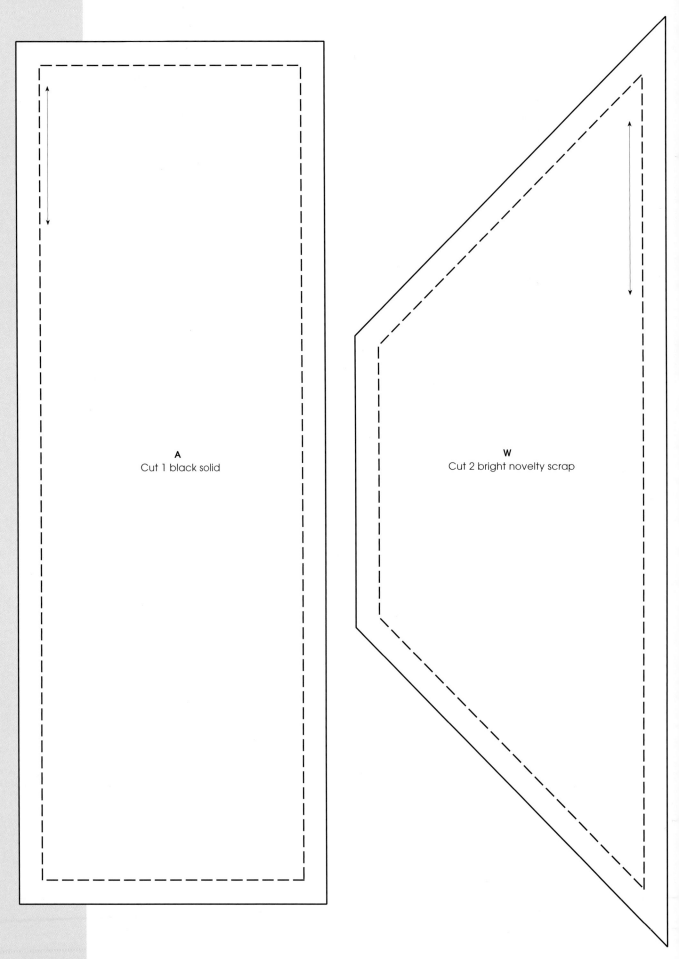

A
Cut 1 black solid

W
Cut 2 bright novelty scrap

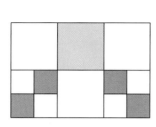

HALF IRISH CHAIN
12" x 8" Block

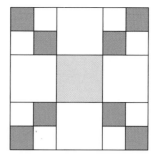

IRISH CHAIN
12" x 12" Block

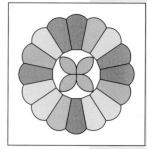

DRESDEN PLATE
12" x 12" Block

Irish Dresden Plate

DESIGN > BARBARA CLAYTON

The Dresden Plate is the perfect pattern for using up lots of scraps. In this quilt, both the blocks and the border shapes will go far toward emptying your scrap basket.

PROJECT NOTE

The quilt shown has a planned scrappy look that uses light and medium shades of blue, green and pink. Because the fabrics are cut in strips to eliminate one step of the cutting/stitching process, the plate pieces in the sample were not cut from hundreds of scraps. If you have a large variety of scraps, this quilt would look lovely with a less planned look.

PROJECT SPECIFICATIONS

Skill Level: Advanced
Quilt Size: Approximately 66½" x 91"
Block Size: 12" x 12" and 12" x 8"
Number of Blocks: 15 and 10

MATERIALS

- ⅛ yard each pink solid and medium blue tonal for petals
- ¼ yard total light blue scraps
- ½ yard total light green and medium blue scraps
- ⅞ yard blue-and-white gingham
- 1 yard medium green tonal
- 1¾ yards total pink scraps
- 5 yards white solid
- Backing 73" x 97"
- Batting 73" x 97"
- Neutral color all-purpose thread
- Quilting thread
- Clear nylon monofilament
- 1½ yards fusible interfacing
- Stylet
- Basic sewing tools and supplies

INSTRUCTIONS

Making Dresden Plate Blocks

Step 1. Cut eight white solid A squares 12½" x 12½" for blocks. Fold and crease squares horizontally, vertically and diagonally to mark block centers.

Step 2. Cut 2½" by fabric width strips as follows: one light blue scrap, four each light green scraps, medium green tonal, blue-and-white gingham and medium blue scraps and 17 pink scraps.

Step 3. Sew a pink strip to a medium green strip with right sides together along length; press seam toward darker strip. Repeat to make four strip sets. Repeat to make one light blue/pink and four sets each light green/pink, gingham/pink and medium blue/pink. Press seams toward darker fabrics.

Step 4. Prepare a template for the B Unit using pattern given.

Step 5. Place the B Unit template on the sewn strips, lining up the straight line between B pieces with the seam between the strips as shown in **Figure 1**. Cut the following B units: eight light blue/pink, 32 gingham/pink, 36 each medium green/pink and light green/pink and 40 medium blue/pink. Set aside 20 each medium green/pink and light green/pink and 24 each gingham/pink and medium blue/pink for borders.

FIGURE 1 Line up the straight line between B pieces with the seam between the strips.

Step 6. Sew a medium green/pink B unit to a light green/pink B unit to make a quarter unit as shown in **Figure 2**. Repeat to make 16 green/pink quarter units, again referring to **Figure 2**. Sew a medium blue/pink B unit to a light blue/pink B unit; repeat for eight quarter units. Repeat with medium blue/pink and gingham/pink B units to make eight quarter units, again referring to **Figure 2**.

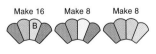

Make 16   Make 8   Make 8

FIGURE 2 Make quarter units as shown.

Step 7. Join two quarter units as shown in **Figure 3**; repeat. Join these halves to complete one Dresden Plate unit, again referring to **Figure 3**. Press joining seams in one direction.

Repeat for four green/pink and four blue/pink Dresden Plate units.

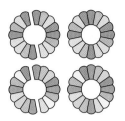

FIGURE 3 Join B units as shown to complete Dresden Plate units.

Step 8. Pin the Dresden Plate units to the lightweight fusible interfacing with the right side of the fabric toward the fusible side of the interfacing. Cut out the interfacing around outside edge of plate units.

Step 9. Stitch around the outside curved edges of the plate units and the inside circle edge using a ¼" seam allowance.

Step 10. Trim away the interfacing in center circle and around outer edge to match the plate unit; clip curves and inverted points.

Step 11. Cut through the center of the interfacing above the B pieces all the way around the plate unit as shown in **Figure 4**; turn right side out through the opening.

FIGURE 4 Cut through the center of the interfacing all the way around.

Step 12. Using a broken pencil or stylet, smooth the curved edges.

Step 13. Center and pin one plate unit to an A square using crease lines as guides for placement as shown in **Figure 5**; press shapes in place to fuse.

FIGURE 5 Center and pin 1 plate unit to an A square using crease lines as guides for placement.

Step 14. Using clear nylon monofilament and a machine blind-hem stitch, sew around the out-

sides together along length; press seams toward darker fabric. Subcut strip sets into (96) 2½" E-F units.

Step 4. To complete one Irish Chain block, join two E-F units as shown in **Figure 6**; press seams in one direction. Repeat for four units.

FIGURE 6 Join 2 E-F units.

Step 5. Arrange the E-F units with C and D squares in rows referring to **Figure 7**. Join in rows; press seams away from C squares. Join the rows to complete one Irish Chain block; press seams toward D row. Repeat for seven blocks.

FIGURE 7 Arrange the E-F units with C and D squares in rows.

Step 6. To make Half Irish Chain blocks, join two E-F units with one D and three C squares as shown in **Figure 8**; press as for whole blocks. Repeat for 10 half blocks.

FIGURE 8 Join 2 E-F units with C and D squares in rows.

Completing the Pieced Center

Step 1. Cut four 8½" x 8½" G squares and six 8½" x 12½" H rectangles white solid.

Step 2. Join two G, one H and two half blocks to make a row as shown in **Figure 9**; repeat for two rows. Press seams toward G and H.

FIGURE 9 Join 2 G, 1 H and 2 half blocks to make a row.

Step 3. Join two half blocks with one Irish Chain block and one each blue and green Dresden Plate blocks to make a row as shown in **Figure 10**; press seams toward Dresden Plate blocks. Repeat to make 3 rows.

side and inside edge of each plate unit.

Step 15. Prepare petal template using pattern given; cut as directed on the piece.

Step 16. Pin the petals to the lightweight fusible interfacing and cut out as for plate units; stitch around outside edges using a ¼" seam allowance. Cut a slit in the interfacing side of each stitched petal; turn right side out. Smooth as for plate units.

Step 17. Center four blue petals in the blue blocks and four pink petals in the green blocks referring to the block drawing for positioning; fuse and stitch in place as for plate units.

Completing the Irish Chain Blocks

Step 1. Cut seven strips white solid 4½" by fabric width; subcut into (58) 4½" C squares.

Step 2. Cut two strips blue-and-white gingham 4½" by fabric width; subcut into (17) 4½" x 4½" D squares.

Step 3. Cut six strips each white solid (E) and medium green tonal (F) 2½" by fabric width. Sew a white strip to a green strip with right

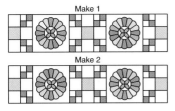

Make 1

Make 2

FIGURE 10 Join 2 half blocks with 1 Irish Chain block and 1 each blue and green Dresden Plate block to make a row.

Step 4. Join two H rectangles with two Irish Chain blocks and one green Dresden Plate block to make a row as shown in **Figure 11**; repeat for another row with a blue block. Press seams toward Dresden Plate blocks.

H

FIGURE 11 Join 2 H with 2 Irish Chain blocks and 1 green Dresden Plate block to make a row.

Step 5. Arrange pieced rows as shown in **Figure 12**; join rows to complete the pieced center.

FIGURE 12 Arrange pieced rows as shown.

Completing the Pieced Border

Step 1. Cut and piece two 8½" x 52½" I strips and two 8½" x 92½" J strips white solid. Sew the I strips to the top and bottom and the J strips to opposite long sides of the pieced center; press seams toward strips.

Step 2. Prepare templates for B and K using patterns given; cut as directed on each piece.

IRISH DRESDEN PLATE Placement Diagram Approximately 66½" x 91"

Step 3. Using B units set aside in Making Dresden Plate Blocks, sew a medium green/ pink B unit to a light green/pink B unit; add a medium green B to the pink end to complete one green shell unit as shown in **Figure 13**; press. Repeat to make 20 units.

Make 24   Make 20

FIGURE 13 Join B units with B to make shell units.

Step 4. Join two medium blue/pink B units and add a gingham B to the pink end to complete one blue shell unit, again referring to **Figure 13**; press. Repeat to make 24 units.

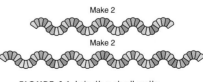

Make 2

Make 2

FIGURE 14 Join the shell units, alternating blue and green shells.

Step 5. Join the shell units, alternating blue and green shells as shown in **Figure 14**. *Note: The blue shells curve outward and the green* *shells curve inward.* You will need two strips with seven blue and six green shells for the side borders and two strips with five blue and four green shells for the top and bottom borders.

Step 6. Sew a medium green KR to a pink K to make a corner unit as shown in **Figure 15**; press. Repeat for four corner units.

FIGURE 15 Complete a corner unit as shown.

Step 7. Join the top and bottom and side border strips with the corner units to make a rectangle as shown in **Figure 16**.

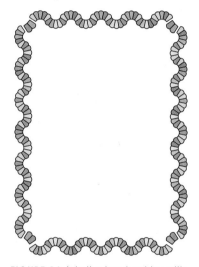

FIGURE 16 Join the border strips with the corner units to make a rectangle.

Step 8. Stitch a turning guideline ¼" from the inside and outside edges all around pieced rectangle.

Step 9. Place the rectangle on the I/J border strips with the innermost green pieces approximately ¾" from the I/J border seam line as shown in **Figure 17**. *Note: Adjust seams between pieces as necessary to make fit.*

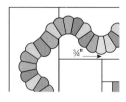

FIGURE 17 Place the innermost green pieces ¾" from the I/J seam line.

Step 10. Fold under the inside raw edges along the stitched guideline and pin in place on border strips, clipping curves as you pin.

Step 11. Stitch the inside edge of the rectangle to the border strips with clear nylon monofilament using a blind-hem stitch as for the Dresden Plate blocks. Trim away the excess white border fabric from behind and beyond the pieced border after stitching is complete as shown in **Figure 18**.

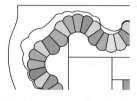

FIGURE 18 Trim excess border from behind and beyond the pieced border.

Finishing the Quilt

Step 1. Lay the batting on a flat surface; lay the prepared backing on the batting right side up. Lay the quilt top right sides together with backing. Smooth layers and baste or pin to hold flat.

Step 2. Sew around the outside curved edges, leaving about a 10" opening for turning.

Step 3. Trim excess batting and backing even with top edges; clip each curve and inverted point. Turn right side out through opening. Smooth edges with stylet.

Step 4. Turn under the edges at the opening ¼" and slipstich opening closed. Lightly press the border edges.

Step 5. Hand- or machine-quilt ¼" from edge of quilt.

Step 6. Hand- or machine-quilt as desired referring to **Figure 19** for suggestions. ◆

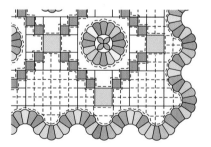

FIGURE 19 Suggested quilting design.

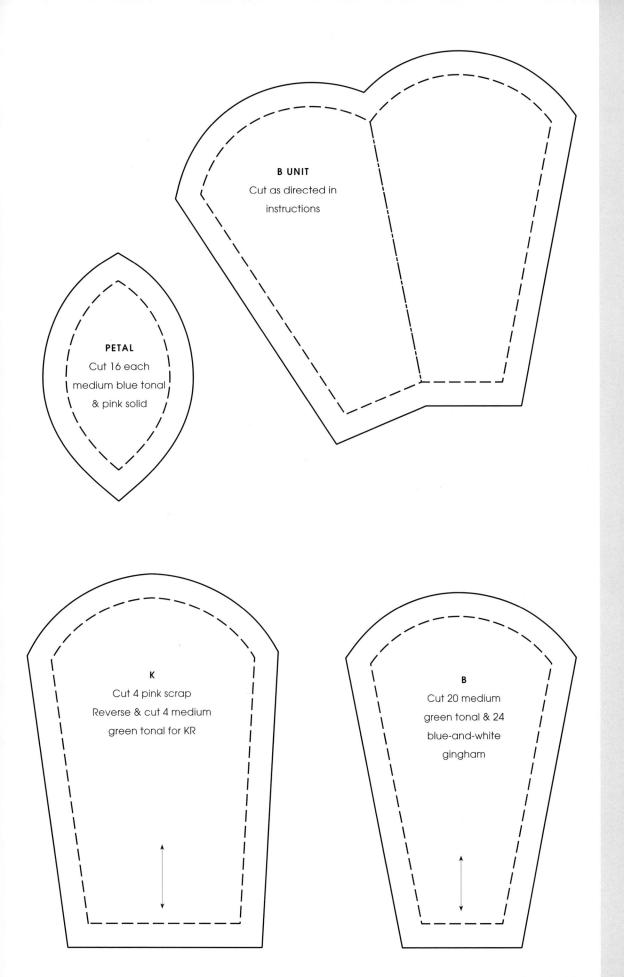

B UNIT
Cut as directed in
instructions

PETAL
Cut 16 each
medium blue tonal
& pink solid

K
Cut 4 pink scrap
Reverse & cut 4 medium
green tonal for KR

B
Cut 20 medium
green tonal & 24
blue-and-white
gingham

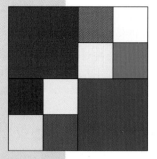

DARK FOUR-PATCH
5" x 5" Block

LIGHT FOUR-PATCH
5" x 5" Block

Christmas Counterchange

DESIGN > JODI WARNER

Select a variety of scraps in Christmas colors and cream to make this very simple Four-Patch design.

PROJECT SPECIFICATIONS

Skill Level: Advanced
Quilt Size: 59" x 69"
Block Size: 5" x 5"
Number of Blocks: 99

MATERIALS

- 7" x 15" scraps of 25 different red/burgundy, green and cream fabrics
- ¼ yard green tonal
- ⅜ yard cream print
- 1½ yards burgundy print
- Backing 65" x 75"
- Batting 65" x 75"
- Neutral color all-purpose thread
- Quilting thread
- Basic tools and supplies

INSTRUCTIONS

Cutting

Step 1. From each red/burgundy and green scrap, cut two 3" x 3" A squares and one 1¾" x 14" B strip.

Step 2. From each cream scrap, cut four 3" x 3" C squares and two 1¾" x 14" D strips.

Step 3. Cut five 1¾" by fabric width strips cream print. Join strips on short ends to make one long strip; press seams to one side. Subcut strip into two 55½" F and two 48" G strips.

Step 4. Cut six 1¼" by fabric width strips green tonal. Join strips on short ends to make one long strip; press seams to one side. Subcut strip into two 58" H and two 49½" I strips.

Step 5. Cut six 5½" by fabric width strips burgundy print. Join strips on short ends to make one long strip; press seams to one side. Subcut strip into four 59½" J strips.

Step 6. Cut seven 2¼" by fabric width burgundy print for binding.

Piecing Blocks

Step 1. Sew a D strip to a B strip to make a strip set; press seams toward B. Subcut strip set into eight 1¾" B-D segments as shown in **Figure 1**. Repeat with all B and D strips.

FIGURE 1 Subcut B-D strip sets into 1¾" segments.

CHRISTMAS COUNTERCHANGE Placement Diagram 59" x 69"

Step 2. To make Dark Four-Patch blocks, sew a green/cream B-D segment to a red/cream B-D segment as shown in **Figure 2**; repeat for 100 units.

FIGURE 2 Sew a green/cream B-D segment to a red/cream B-D segment.

Step 3. Sew a red/burgundy A to a B-D unit as shown in **Figure 3**; repeat for 50 units. Repeat with a green A and a B-D unit, again referring to Figure 3 to make 50 units. Press seams toward A.

FIGURE 3 Sew A to B-D segments.

Step 4. Join one unit of each color combination to complete one Dark Four-Patch block referring to **Figure 4**; repeat for 50 blocks. Press seams in one direction.

FIGURE 4 Join units to complete a Dark Four-Patch block.

Step 5. To make Light Four-Patch blocks, join two red/cream B-D segments as shown in **Figure 5**; repeat for 49 units. Join two green/cream B-D segments, again referring to Figure 5; repeat for 49 units.

FIGURE 5 Join B-D segments as shown.

Step 6. Sew a C square to each B-D unit as shown in **Figure 6**; press seams toward C. Join the units to complete one Light Four-Patch block as shown in **Figure 7**; repeat for 49 blocks.

FIGURE 6 Sew a C square to each B-D unit.

FIGURE 7 Join the units to complete a Light Four-Patch block.

Completing the Top
Step 1. Join four Light Four-Patch blocks and five Dark Four-Patch blocks to make a row referring to **Figure 8**; press seams toward Dark Four-Patch blocks. Repeat for six rows.
Step 2. Join four Dark Four-Patch blocks and five Light Four-Patch blocks to make a row, again referring to **Figure 8**; press seams toward Dark Four-Patch blocks. Repeat for five rows.

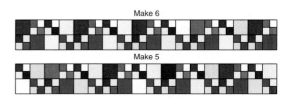

FIGURE 8 Join blocks to make rows.

Step 3. Join the rows referring to the Placement Diagram to complete the pieced top; press seams in one direction.
Step 4. Sew an F strip to opposite sides and a G strip to the top and bottom of the pieced center; press seams toward strips.

Step 5. Sew an H strip to opposite sides and an I strip to the top and bottom of the pieced center; press seams toward H and I strips.

Step 6. Sew a J strip to opposite sides and to the top and bottom of the pieced center; press seams toward J strips.

Finishing the Quilt

Step 1. Sandwich the batting between the completed top and prepared backing piece; pin or baste to hold.

Step 2. Hand- or machine-quilt as desired. **Note:** *The quilting design given was machine-quilted in the J border strips on the sample quilt.*

Step 3. Trim batting and backing even with the quilted top.

Step 4. Join the binding strips on short ends with a diagonal seam to make a long strip; press seams toward one side.

Step 5. Press the strip in half along length with wrong sides together to complete the binding strip. Bind edges of quilt to finish. ◆

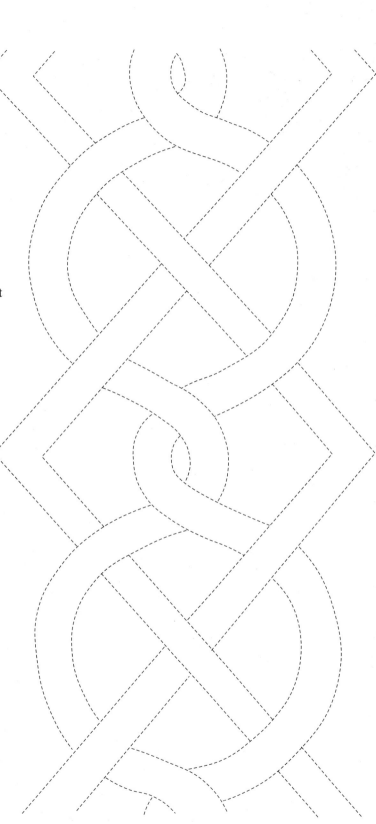

BORDER QUILTING DESIGN

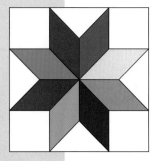

STAR
14" x 14" Block

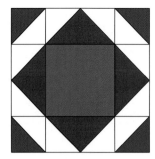

SQUARE-IN-A-SQUARE
14" x 14" Block

Field of Diamonds

DESIGN > JUDITH SANDSTROM

Show your patriotic spirit in this scrappy red, white and blue quilt.

PROJECT SPECIFICATIONS

Skill Level: Beginner
Quilt Size: 84" x 98"
Block Size: 14" x 14"
Number of Blocks: 30

MATERIALS

- ½ yard each 10 patriotic prints
- ¾ yard red print for binding
- 1 yard red tonal
- 2½ yards navy print
- 3¾ yards cream tonal
- Backing 90" x 104"
- Batting 90" x 104"
- Neutral color and navy all-purpose thread
- Quilting thread
- 1 package ¼"-wide iron-on adhesive
- Basic tools and supplies

INSTRUCTIONS

Cutting

Step 1. Cut two 14½" strips along the length of the cream tonal; subcut strips into (15) 14½"

A squares. Fold and crease each A square to mark centers.

Step 2. From each of the 10 patriotic prints, cut two 3⅛" by fabric width B strips and two 7½" x 7½" F squares. Cut one end of each B strip at a 45-degree angle and subcut into (12) 3⅛" diamond shapes referring to **Figure 1**.

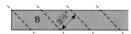

FIGURE 1 Cut B strips at a 45-degree angle; subcut into 3⅛" B diamonds.

Step 3. Cut three 4⅜" strips along the length of the remaining cream tonal; subcut strips into (90) 4⅜" C squares. Cut each square in half on one diagonal to make 180 C triangles.

Step 4. Cut two 7½" x 70½" G strips and two 7½" x 84½" H strips along the length of the navy print.

Step 5. Cut two 4⅜" D strips along the length of the remaining navy print; subcut strips into (30) 4⅜" D squares. Cut each square in half on one diagonal to make 60 D triangles.

Step 6. Cut five 5⅞" by fabric width strips red tonal; subcut strips into (30) 5⅞" E squares. Cut each square in half on one diagonal to make 60 E triangles.

Step 7. Cut nine 2¼" by fabric width strips red print for binding.

Completing Star Blocks

Step 1. Pair B diamonds right sides together and chain-stitch to make B units as shown in **Figure 2**; repeat for all B units. Press seams open.

FIGURE 2 Chain-stitch B units in pairs.

Step 2. Randomly stitch four B units together to complete a star shape pressing all seams open.

Step 3. Bond iron-on adhesive strips to the wrong side of the outer edges of each star shape as shown in **Figure 3**; remove paper backing.

FIGURE 3 Bond iron-on adhesive strips to the wrong side of the outer edges of star shapes.

Step 4. Center one star shape on an A square and fuse in place to complete one Star block; repeat for 15 blocks.

Step 5. Machine-stitch around star shapes using a medium-width satin stitch and navy all-purpose thread.

Piecing Square-in-a-Square Blocks

Step 1. Set aside four F squares for border corners and one for another project.

Step 2. Sew C to D along the diagonal as shown in **Figure 4**; press seam toward D. Repeat for four C-D units.

FIGURE 4 Sew C to D.   FIGURE 5 Sew C to adjacent sides of E.

Step 3. Sew C to adjacent sides of E as shown in **Figure 5**; press seams toward C. Repeat for four C-E units.

Step 4. Sew C-E to opposite sides of F to make a row as shown in **Figure 6**; press seams toward F.

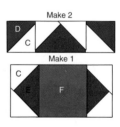

FIGURE 6 Join units to make rows.

Step 5. Sew C-D to opposite ends of a C-E unit to make a row, again referring to **Figure 6**; press seams toward C-D. Repeat for two rows.

Step 6. Join the rows to complete one Square-in-a-Square block as shown in **Figure 7**; press seams in one direction. Repeat for 15 blocks.

FIGURE 7 Join rows to complete 1 block.

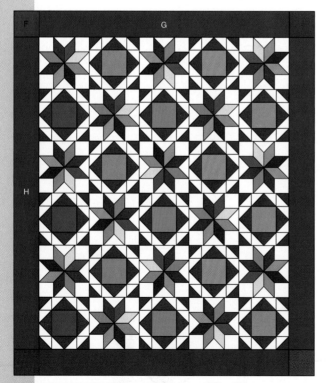

FIELD OF DIAMONDS Placement Diagram 84" x 98"

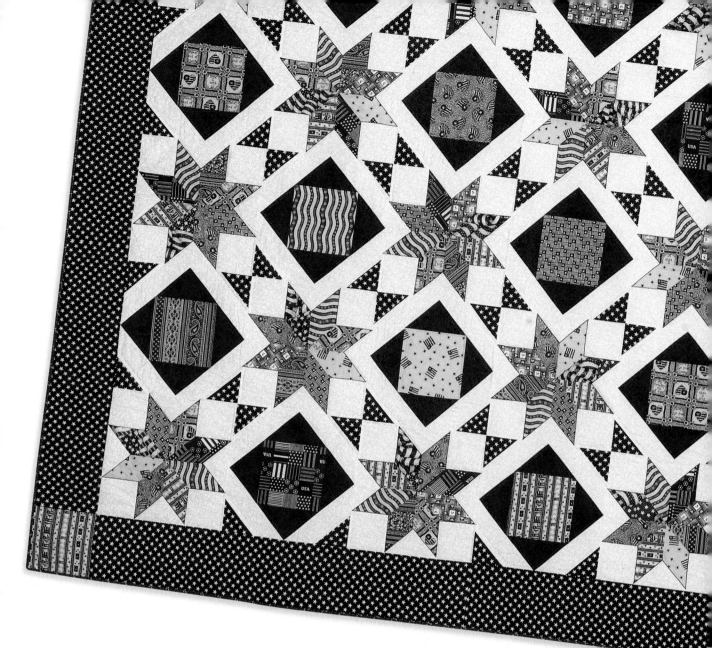

Completing the Top

Step 1. Join three Star blocks with two Square-in-a-Square blocks to make a row; repeat for three rows. Press seams toward Square-in-a-Square blocks.

Step 2. Join three Square-in-a-Square blocks with two Star blocks to make a row; repeat for three rows. Press seams toward Square-in-a-Square blocks.

Step 3. Join rows referring to the Placement Diagram for positioning of rows; press seams in one direction.

Step 4. Sew a G strip to the top and bottom of the pieced center; press seams toward G.

Step 5. Sew an F square to each end of each H strip; press seam toward H. Sew the F-H strips to opposite long sides of the pieced center to complete the top; press seams toward F-H strips.

Finishing the Quilt

Step 1. Sandwich the batting between the completed top and prepared backing piece; pin or baste to hold.

Step 2. Hand- or machine-quilt as desired.

Step 3. Trim batting and backing even with the quilted top.

Step 4. Join the binding strips on short ends with a diagonal seam to make a long strip; press seams toward one side.

Step 5. Press the strip in half along length with wrong sides together to complete the binding strip. Bind edges of quilt to finish. ◆

A BLOCK
14" x 14" Block

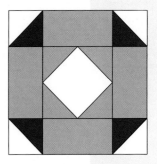

B BLOCK
14" x 14" Block

Purple Passion

DESIGN > JUDITH SANDSTROM

Choose a variety of same-color prints to create a
monochromatic scrappy quilt.

PROJECT SPECIFICATIONS

Skill Level: Beginner
Quilt Size: 84" x 98"
Block Size: 14" x 14"
Number of Blocks: 30

MATERIALS

- ½ yard each 8 lavender prints
- 1¾ yards dark purple floral
- 2¼ yards dark purple print
- 2⅓ yards white tonal
- Backing 90" x 104"
- Batting 90" x 104"
- Neutral color all-purpose thread
- Quilting thread
- Basic tools and supplies

INSTRUCTIONS

Cutting

Step 1. Cut (11) 5½" by fabric width strips
white tonal; subcut strips into (75) 5½"
B squares.

Step 2. Cut four 4⅜" by fabric width strips
white tonal; subcut into (30) 4⅜" F squares. Cut
each square in half on one diagonal to make 60
F triangles.

Step 3. Cut three 8¼" by fabric width strips
dark purple floral; subcut strips into (15) 8¼"
C squares. Cut each square on both diagonals
to make 60 C triangles.

Step 4. Cut seven 4⅜" by fabric width strips
dark purple floral; subcut strips into (60) 4⅜"
D squares. Cut each square on one diagonal to
make 120 D triangles.

Step 5. Cut three 5½" by fabric width strips
dark purple print; subcut strips into (15) 5½"
A squares.

Step 6. Cut eight 4" by fabric width strips dark
purple print for H and I borders.

Step 7. Cut four 7½" x 7½" J squares dark
purple print.

Step 8. From each of the eight lavender prints
cut two 4" by fabric width strips; subcut each
strip to make (10) 7½" G rectangles of each
print. Cut one strip each 4⅜" by fabric width;
from each strip cut four 4⅜" E squares and

three 4" x 7½" G rectangles. Cut each E square in half on one diagonal to make eight E triangles from each fabric.

Step 9. Cut nine 2¼" by fabric width strips dark purple print for binding.

Making A Blocks

Step 1. To piece one A block, sew B to opposite sides of A and add D as shown in **Figure 1**; press seams away from B.

FIGURE 1 Sew B to opposite sides of A; add D.

Step 2. Sew C to opposite sides of B and add D as shown in **Figure 2**; press seams toward B. Repeat for two units.

FIGURE 2 Sew C to opposite sides of B; add D.

Step 3. Sew a B-C-D unit to opposite sides of the A-B-D unit to complete one A block referring to **Figure 3**; press seams away from A-B-D unit. Repeat for 15 blocks.

FIGURE 3 Sew a B-C-D unit to opposite sides of the A-B-D unit to complete 1 A block.

Making B Blocks

Step 1. To piece one B block, sew D to F along the diagonals; repeat for four D-F units. Press seams toward D.

Step 2. Select four same-fabric E and G pieces. Sew E to each side of B as shown in **Figure 4**; press seams toward E.

FIGURE 4 Sew E to each side of B.

Step 3. Sew G to opposite sides of the B-E unit as shown in **Figure 5**; press seams toward G.

FIGURE 5 Sew G to E-B.

Step 4. Sew a D-F unit to opposite ends of G as shown in **Figure 6**; press seams toward G. Repeat for two units.

FIGURE 6 Sew a D-F unit to opposite ends of G.

Step 5. Sew a D-F-G unit to opposite sides of the B-E-G unit to complete one B block referring to **Figure 7**; press seams toward D-F-G. Repeat for 15 blocks.

FIGURE 7 Sew a D-F-G unit to opposite sides of the B-E-G unit to complete 1 B block.

Completing the Top
Step 1. Join three A blocks with two B blocks to make a row; press seams toward A blocks. Repeat for three rows.
Step 2. Join three B blocks with two A blocks to make a row; press seams toward A blocks. Repeat for three rows.
Step 3. Join the rows referring to the Placement Diagram for positioning; press seams in one direction.
Step 4. Join the H and I strips on short ends to make one long strip; press. Cut strip into two 4" x 84½" H strips and two 4" x 70½" I strips.
Step 5. Join 12 G rectangles on short ends to make a side strip; sew to an H strip. Press seams toward H. Repeat for two G-H strips.
Step 6. Sew a G-H strip to opposite sides of the pieced center; press seams toward H.

PURPLE PASSION Placement Diagram 84" x 98"

Step 7. Join 10 G rectangles on short ends to make a top strip; sew to an I strip. Press seams toward I. Repeat for two G-I strips.
Step 8. Sew a J square to each end of each G-I strip; press seams toward G-I.
Step 9. Sew a G-I-J strip to the top and bottom of the pieced center with the G sides toward the outside; press seams toward I to complete the pieced top.

Finishing the Quilt
Step 1. Sandwich the batting between the completed top and prepared backing piece; pin or baste to hold.
Step 2. Hand- or machine-quilt as desired.
Step 3. Trim batting and backing even with the quilted top.
Step 4. Join the binding strips on short ends with a diagonal seam to make a long strip; press seams toward one side.
Step 5. Press the strip in half along length with wrong sides together to complete the binding strip. Bind edges of quilt to finish. ◆

SUNNY LANES VARIATION A
20" x 20" Block

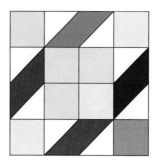

SUNNY LANES VARIATION B
20" x 20" Block

Sunlit Scraps

DESIGN > SUE HARVEY

Careful placement of light, medium and dark values creates the design in this bed-size flannel quilt.

PROJECT SPECIFICATIONS

Skill Level: Beginner
Quilt Size: 95" x 95"
Block Size: 20" x 20"
Number of Blocks: 16

MATERIALS

- ⅞ yard cream tonal flannel for border
- ⅞ yard total dark flannel binding fabrics
- 3½ yards total light flannel scraps
- 4 yards total medium flannel scraps
- 5½ yards total dark flannel scraps
- Backing 101" x 101"
- Batting 101" x 101"
- Neutral color all-purpose thread
- Quilting thread
- Basic tools and supplies

INSTRUCTIONS
Cutting

Step 1. Cut 128 squares 5½" x 5½" medium scraps for A.

Step 2. Cut 32 rectangles 5½" x 10½" light scraps for B.

Step 3. Cut 64 squares 5½" x 5½" light scraps for E.

Step 4. Cut 64 squares 5½" x 5½" dark scraps for C.

Step 5. Cut 32 rectangles 5½" x 10½" dark scraps for D.

Step 6. Cut eight strips 3" by fabric width cream tonal; set aside for F and G borders.

Step 7. Cut 10 strips 2½" by fabric width from binding fabrics.

Step 8. Cut remaining dark scraps in 5½"-wide, random-length strips; set aside for H and I borders.

Piecing Blocks

Step 1. Draw a diagonal line from corner to corner on the wrong side of each C and E square.

Step 2. Place a C square right sides together on one end of a B rectangle; stitch on the marked

line, trim seam allowance to ¼" and press C to the right side as shown in **Figure 1**.

FIGURE 1 Complete 1 B-C unit.

Step 3. Repeat on the remaining end of B to complete one B-C unit, again referring to **Figure 1**. Repeat to make 16 B-C units.
Step 4. Repeat Steps 2 and 3 to make 16 reversed B-C units as shown in **Figure 2**.

FIGURE 2 Complete reversed B-C
units and D-E and reversed D-E units.

Step 5. Repeat Steps 2 and 3 using D and E pieces to complete 16 each D-E and reversed D-E units, again referring to **Figure 2**.
Step 6. Join two A squares to make a row; press seam to one side. Repeat for 32 A rows.

Step 7. Join two A rows to complete a center unit as shown in **Figure 3**; press seam to one side. Repeat for 16 center units.

FIGURE 3 Complete a center unit.

Step 8. To piece one Sunny Lanes Variation A block, sew a reversed B-C unit to opposite sides of a center unit to make a row as shown in **Figure 4**; press seams toward B-C.

FIGURE 4 Sew reversed B-C units
to opposite sides of a center unit.

Step 9. Sew an A square to each end of a B-C unit to make a row as shown in **Figure 5**; press seams toward B-C. Repeat for two rows.

FIGURE 5 Sew A to each end of
a B-C unit.

Step 10. Join the rows to complete one A block as shown in **Figure 6**; press seams toward the outer row. Repeat for 16 A blocks.

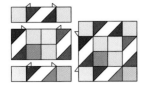

FIGURE 6 Complete 1 Sunny Lanes Variation A block.

Step 11. Repeat Steps 7–9 to complete one Sunny Lanes Variation B block using D-E and reversed D-E units as shown in **Figure 7**, except press seams toward the A center unit, the A squares and the center rows; repeat for 16 B blocks.

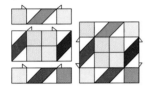

FIGURE 7 Complete 1 Sunny Lanes Variation B block.

Completing the Top

Step 1. Join two A blocks with two B blocks to make a row as shown in **Figure 8**; repeat for four rows. Press seams in one direction in each row.

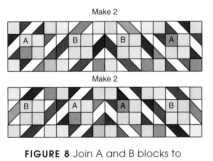

FIGURE 8 Join A and B blocks to make rows.

Step 2. Join the rows to complete the pieced center referring to the Placement Diagram for positioning of rows. Press seams open between rows.

Step 3. Join the F/G border strips on short ends to make a long strip; cut into two 80½"-long F strips and two 85½"-long G strips.

SUNLIT SCRAPS Placement Diagram 95" x 95"

Step 4. Sew the F strips to opposite sides and the G strips to the remaining sides; press seams toward strips.

Step 5. Join the H/I strips on short ends to make a strip 370" long; cut into two 85½"-long H strips and two 95½"-long I strips.

Step 6. Sew the H strips to opposite sides and the I strips to the remaining sides; press seams toward strips to complete the top.

Finishing the Quilt

Step 1. Sandwich the batting between the completed top and prepared backing piece; pin or baste to hold.

Step 2. Hand- or machine-quilt as desired.

Step 3. Trim batting and backing even with the quilted top.

Step 4. Join the binding strips on short ends with a diagonal seam to make a long strip; press seams toward one side.

Step 5. Press the strip in half along length with wrong sides together to complete the binding strip. Bind edges of quilt to finish. ◆

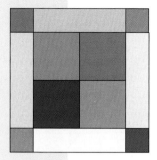

LARGE FOUR-PATCH
6" x 6" Block

Blueberries & Cream

DESIGN > JULIE WEAVER

Navy blue and cream fabrics form a rich contrast in

this large bed-size quilt.

PROJECT NOTES

The instructions are given for this quilt in such a way that every square is cut individually. However, strip piecing could be used, depending on the size of one's scraps. This quilt would lend itself nicely to any two-color scheme.

PROJECT SPECIFICATIONS

Skill Level: Intermediate
Quilt Size: Approximately 79" x 101½"
Block Size: 6" x 6"
Number of Blocks: 83

MATERIALS

- 3 yards blue stripe for second border
- 4½ yards total assorted cream/beige scraps
- 4½ yards total assorted blue scraps
- Backing 85" x 107"
- Batting 85" x 107"
- Neutral color all-purpose thread
- Quilting thread
- Basic sewing tools and supplies

INSTRUCTIONS

Making Large Four-Patch Blocks

Step 1. From assorted blue scraps, cut a total of (332) 2½" x 2½" A squares.

Step 2. Referring to **Figure 1**, join four A squares to make an A unit; repeat for 83 A units. Press seams in one direction.

FIGURE 1 Join 4 A squares
to make an A unit.

Step 3. From assorted blue scraps, cut a total of (332) 1½" x 1½" B squares.

Step 4. From assorted cream/beige scraps, cut a total of (332) 1½" x 4½" C rectangles.

Step 5. To complete one Large Four-Patch block, sew C to opposite sides of an A unit as shown in **Figure 2**; press seams toward C.

FIGURE 2 Sew C to opposite
sides of an A unit.

Step 6. Sew B to opposite ends of two C pieces; press seams toward C. Sew a B-C unit to the remaining sides of the A-C unit as shown in **Figure 3** to complete one block; press seams toward B-C. Repeat for 83 blocks.

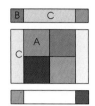

FIGURE 3 Sew a B-C unit to the remaining sides of the A-C unit.

Making Sashing Units

Step 1. From assorted blue scraps, cut a total of (328) 1½" x 1½" D squares.

Step 2. Join four D squares as in Step 2 for A units; repeat for 82 sashing units.

Step 3. From assorted cream/beige scraps, cut a total of (188) 2½" x 6½" E rectangles.

Completing the Top

Step 1. Arrange Large Four-Patch blocks with sashing units and E rectangles in diagonal rows as shown in **Figure 4**.

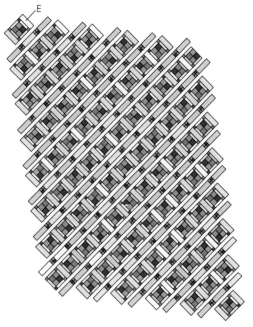

FIGURE 4 Arrange blocks, sashing units and E rectangles in diagonal rows.

Step 2. When satisfied with arrangement, join Large Four-Patch blocks with E in diagonal rows. Join sashing units with E in diagonal rows. Press seams toward E.

Step 3. Join completed rows; press seams away from E.

Step 4. Referring to **Figure 5**, trim ¼" past the center of each edge piece to make square edges. *Note: After trimming, the outer edges are now on the bias and will stretch easily until the first border is added.*

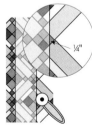

FIGURE 5 Trim ¼" past the center of each edge piece to make square edges.

Step 5. To make F and G borders, cut 1½" x 11" strips from assorted blue scraps.

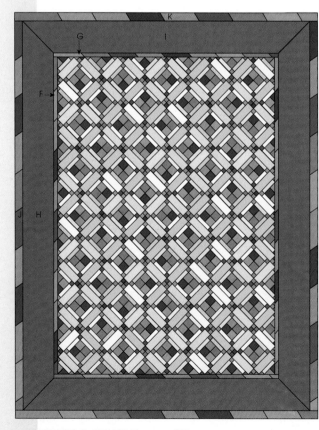

BLUEBERRIES & CREAM Placement Diagram
Approximately 79" x 101½"

Step 6. Measure the center of the quilt from side to side and top to bottom to determine the lengths needed for border strips. *Note: The size should be approximately 57½" x 80".*

Step 7. Referring to **Figure 6**, sew strips diagonally end to end until you have a strip long enough to equal the measurements taken in Step 6. Cut two F strips for opposite long sides and two G strips for the top and bottom. Sew F strips to opposite long sides and G strips to the top and bottom of the pieced center; press seams toward strips.

FIGURE 6 Join strips end to end as shown.

Step 8. Cut nine 8½" by fabric width strips blue stripe; join on short ends to make one long strip. Cut two 100" H strips and two 80" I strips.

Step 9. Sew H to opposite long sides and I to the top and bottom, mitering corners. Trim corner mitered seam to ¼"; press seam open.

Step 10. Cut 2½" x 14½" strips from assorted blue scraps. Repeat Steps 6 and 7 to make J and K strips and sew J to opposite sides and K to the top and bottom of the pieced center to complete the top.

Finishing the Quilt

Step 1. Sandwich the batting between the completed top and prepared backing; pin or baste layers together to hold.

Step 2. Hand- or machine-quilt as desired. When quilting is complete, trim batting and backing even with top; remove pins or basting.

Step 3. Cut nine 2¼" by fabric width strips blue stripe. Join the strips on short ends to make one long strip. Fold the strip in half along length with wrong sides together; press.

Step 4. Sew binding to quilt edges, mitering corners and overlapping ends. Fold binding to the backside and stitch in place. ◆

Which Way Home?

DESIGN > CHRISTINE SCHULTZ

Uneven Flying Geese find their way across this table runner.

PROJECT SPECIFICATIONS

Skill Level: Advanced
Runner Size: 58¼" x 16¼"

MATERIALS

- Random scraps of light and dark fabrics
- ⅔ yard border and binding fabric
- 2 border stripe fabric strips 1½" x 48" (H)
- 1 border stripe fabric strip 1¾" x 55" (I)
- Backing 64" x 22"
- Batting 64" x 22"
- Neutral color all-purpose thread
- Quilting thread
- Basic sewing tools and supplies

INSTRUCTIONS

Step 1. Prepare foundation copies as directed on pattern.

Step 2. Cut (10) 2½" x 2½" D squares, one 2½" x 4½" E rectangle, one 2½" x 1½" F rectangle and one 2½" x 6½" G rectangle light scraps.

Step 3. Using random scraps of dark for A and light for B and C, make 13 complete Flying Geese strips using paper foundation patterns, beginning at one end of the strip and continuing the piecing sequence in numerical order referring to **Figure 1**.

FIGURE 1 Join Flying Geese units to make strips as shown.

Step 4. Press finished pieced strips without steam and trim to outer cutting line. Do not remove paper.

Step 5. Referring to Figure 1, join four pairs of pieced Flying Geese strips together on the short ends to make four 26-unit strips. Remove four geese units from one end of one strip to make a 22-unit strip.

Step 6. Remove six geese units from one 13-unit strip to make a seven-unit strip.

Step 7. Join the units with D, E, F and G to make rows as shown in **Figure 2**.

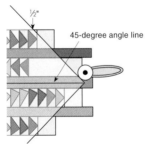

FIGURE 2 Join the geese units with D, E, F and G as shown to make rows.

Step 8. Fold each row and each H and I strip and crease to mark the centers. Align centers of rows and H and I strips as shown in **Figure 3**; pin and stitch. *Note: Adjust strips as necessary to align Flying Geese units across the width of the runner, again referring to **Figure 3**. The ends of the strips will be staggered.* Press seams toward H and I strips.

FIGURE 3 Align centers of rows and H and I strips.

Step 9. Trim ends of pieced runner top by aligning the 45-degree diagonal line of a rotary ruler with the middle of the center border strip and the two adjacent sides of the ruler at least ½" beyond the outer side of the last goose in each pieced strip as shown in **Figure 4**; trim to make angled ends.

45-degree angle line

½"

FIGURE 4 Cut angled ends at a 45-degree angle as shown.

Step 10. Cut two 3" by fabric width J strips and four 3" x 14" K strips from border fabric.

Step 11. Center and sew a J strip to opposite long sides of the pieced center, stopping stitching at the end of the seam allowance and leaving strip extending on each end as shown in **Figure 5**; press seams toward J. Repeat with K strips on each end referring to **Figure 6**.

FIGURE 5 Sew J strips to sides, extending at ends and stopping stitching ¼" from end of seam as shown.

FIGURE 6 Sew K strips to ends.

Step 12. Miter corners at end points as shown in **Figure 7**; trim mitered seams to ¼" and press open. Stitch angled corners at side edges as shown in **Figure 8**; trim angled seams to ¼" and press open.

FIGURE 7 Miter end corners as shown.

FIGURE 8 Stitch angled corners at side edges.

Step 13. Remove paper foundations.

Step 14. Sandwich the batting between the completed top and prepared backing; pin or baste layers together to hold.

Step 15. Hand- or machine-quilt as desired. When quilting is complete, trim batting and backing even with top; remove pins or basting.

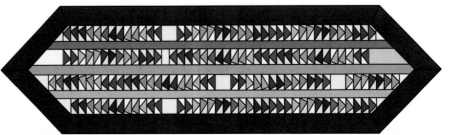

WHICH WAY HOME? Placement Diagram 58¼" x 16¼"

Note: *The quilting design used on the sample is marked on the foundation pattern.*

Step 16. Cut six 1¼" by fabric width strips from binding fabric. Join strips on short ends to make one long strip. Fold one long edge under ¼"; press.

Step 17. Sew binding to quilt edges, mitering corners and overlapping ends. Fold binding to the backside and hand-stitch in place to finish. ◆

Match lines to make complete pattern

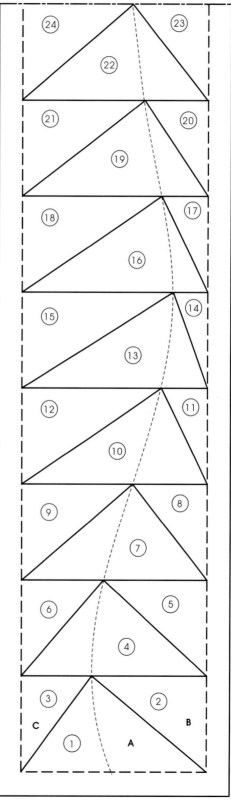

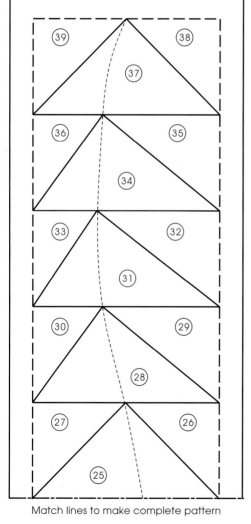

Match lines to make complete pattern

FLYING GEESE FOUNDATION

Make 13 photocopies

CHAINED LIGHTNING
12" x 12" Block

Chained Lightning

DESIGN > PAT CAMPBELL

The white background of this runner ties all the scrap pieces together.

PROJECT SPECIFICATIONS

Skill Level: Beginner
Runner Size: 40" x 16"
Block Size: 12" x 12"
Number of Blocks: 3

MATERIALS

- Scraps dark fabrics
- ¼ yard dark fabric for binding
- 1 yard white solid
- Backing 46" x 22"
- Batting 46" x 22"
- Neutral color all-purpose thread
- Quilting thread
- Basic sewing tools and supplies

INSTRUCTIONS

Step 1. Make 12 photocopies of the foundation pattern given on page 85.

Step 2. Using dark scraps and white solid, cut pieces at least ¼" larger all around than corresponding spaces on the foundation pattern.

Step 3. Pin piece 1 to the unmarked side of a foundation pattern to cover the number 1 space. Pin piece 2 to piece 1 with right sides together referring to **Figure 1**. Turn paper over and stitch on the line between pieces 1 and 2, again referring to **Figure 1**.

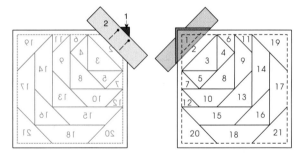

FIGURE 1 Pin piece 2 to piece 1 with right sides together; turn over and stitch on line 1-2.

Step 4. Turn paper over, trim seam to ¼" and press piece 2 to the right side as shown in **Figure 2**. Continue to add pieces in numerical order referring to foundation pattern for color. Repeat for 12 units.

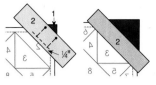

FIGURE 2 Turn paper over, trim seam to ¼" and press piece 2 to the right side.

Step 5. Trim excess fabrics even with outside solid line of foundation papers as shown in **Figure 3**.

FIGURE 3 Trim excess fabrics even with outside solid line of foundation paper.

Step 6. Arrange four units as shown in **Figure 4**. Join two units and press; repeat. Join the pieced units to complete one block; repeat for three blocks.

FIGURE 4 Join units as shown.

Step 7. Join the blocks; press seams in one direction.

Step 8. Cut two 2½" x 36½" A strips and two 2½" x 16½" B strips white solid.

Step 9. Sew an A strip to opposite long sides and a B strip to opposite short ends of the pieced center; press seams toward strips. Remove paper backing from all pieces.

Step 10. Sandwich the batting between the completed top and prepared backing; pin or baste layers together to hold.

Step 11. Hand- or machine-quilt as desired. When quilting is complete, trim batting and backing even with top; remove pins or basting.

Step 12. Cut three 2¼" by fabric width strips dark fabric for binding. Join the strips on short ends to make one long strip. Fold the strip in half along length with wrong sides together; press.

Step 13. Sew binding to quilt edges, mitering corners and overlapping ends. Fold binding to the backside and stitch in place to finish. ◆

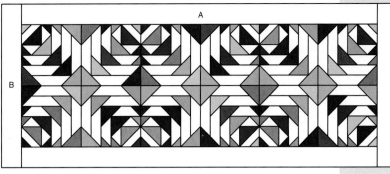

CHAINED LIGHTNING Placement Diagram 40" x 16"

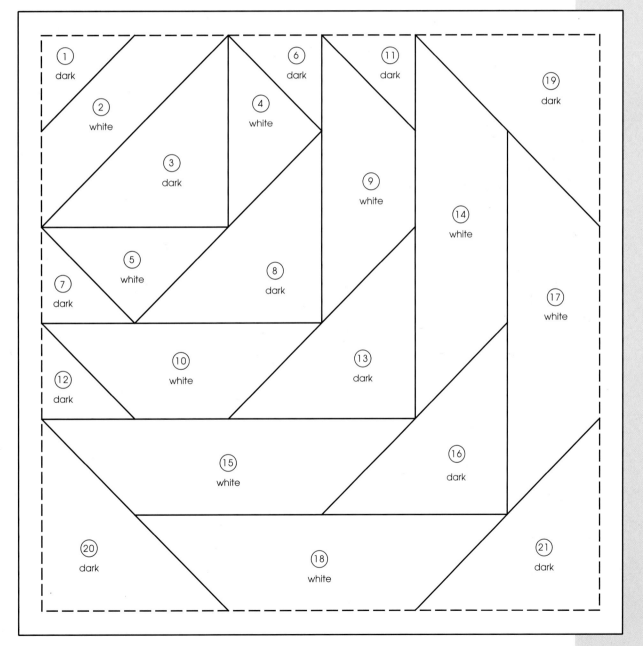

FOUNDATION PATTERN

Make 12 photocopies

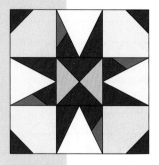

JUBILEE
12" x 12" Block

Plaid
Jubilee

DESIGN > RHONDA TAYLOR

Combine lots of plaids and stripes in this folk-art table runner.

PROJECT SPECIFICATIONS

Skill Level: Intermediate
Runner Size: 44" x 20"
Block Size: 12" x 12"
Number of Blocks: 3

MATERIALS

- 1 fat quarter each 4 cream/tan tonals
- 1 fat quarter each 6 different plaids (fabrics 1–6)
- 1 fat quarter light plaid (fabric 7)
- ⅓ yard dark purple plaid (fabric 9)
- 1 yard rust plaid (fabric 8)
- Backing 50" x 26"
- Batting 50" x 26"
- Black and neutral color all-purpose thread
- Quilting thread
- 1¼ yards lightweight interfacing or paper for foundations
- ¼ yard fusible web
- ½ yard fabric stabilizer
- Basic tools and supplies

INSTRUCTIONS

Cutting

Step 1. Transfer E foundation patterns, found on page 90, to paper or lightweight interfacing as directed on pattern for number of copies.

Step 2. Cut fabric pieces to fit foundation pieces 1–4, adding a ¼" seam allowance around each piece and referring to foundation pattern for color.

Step 3. Cut 4½" x 4½" A squares as follows: two each fabrics 2–6, four fabric 7, six fabric 1 and eight fabric 9. *Note: Refer to Figure 10 and the Color Key for fabric arrangement on project to assign specific numbers to fabrics 1–6.*

Step 4. Cut two 2" by fabric width strips rust plaid; subcut strips into (32) 2" B squares.

Step 5. Cut two 5¼" x 5¼" squares each light plaid (C) and rust plaid (D); cut each square in half on both diagonals to make eight each C and D triangles. Set aside two each C and D triangles for another project.

Step 6. Cut six squares each of two cream/tan tonals 4½" x 4½" for F.

Step 7. Cut four 2¼" by fabric width strips rust plaid for binding.

Piecing Blocks

Step 1. Place piece 1 on the unmarked side of a foundation pattern; pin piece 2 right sides together with piece 1 on the 1-2 line. Turn paper over and stitch on the line between pieces 1 and 2 as shown in **Figure 1**.

FIGURE 1 Turn paper over and stitch on the line between pieces 1 and 2.

Step 2. Turn foundation over; press piece 2 to the right side and add piece 3 and then piece 4 to complete an E unit as shown in **Figure 2**. Repeat for 12 E units.

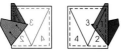

FIGURE 2 Add pieces 3 and 4 to complete an E unit.

Step 3. Sew a C triangle to a D triangle as shown in **Figure 3**; press seams toward D. Repeat for six C-D units.

FIGURE 3 Sew a C triangle to a D triangle.

Step 4. Join two C-D units to complete a block center as shown in **Figure 4**; repeat for three block centers. Press seams in one direction.

FIGURE 4 Join 2 C-D units to complete a block center.

Step 5. Draw a line from corner to corner on the wrong side of each B square.

Step 6. Place a B square on one corner of an F square as shown in **Figure 5**; stitch on the marked line. Trim seam allowance to ¼" and press B to the right side to complete a B-F unit referring to **Figure 6**; repeat for 12 B-F units.

FIGURE 5 Place a B square on 1 corner of an F square.

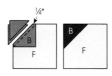

FIGURE 6 Trim seam allowance to ¼" and press B to the right side to complete a B-F unit.

Step 7. To complete one block, join two B-F units with an E unit to make a row referring to **Figure 7**; repeat for two rows. Press seams toward B-F units.

FIGURE 7 Join 2 B-F units with an E unit to make a row.

Step 8. Join two E units with a center C-D unit to make a row as shown in **Figure 8**.

FIGURE 8 Join 2 E units with a center C-D unit.

Step 9. Join the rows as shown in **Figure 9** to complete one block; repeat for three blocks. Press seams in one direction.

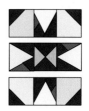

FIGURE 9 Join the rows to complete 1 block.

Completing the Top

Step 1. Join the three pieced blocks referring to the Placement Diagram and project photo for positioning; press seams in one direction.

Step 2. Lay out the A squares around the pieced block center referring to **Figure 10** and the Color Key for arrangement.

FIGURE 10 Lay out the A squares around the pieced block center.

COLOR KEY
- Fabric 1 (green plaid)
- Fabric 2
- Fabric 3
- Fabric 4
- Fabric 5
- Fabric 6
- Fabric 7 (light plaid)
- Fabric 8 (rust plaid)
- Fabric 9 (dark purple plaid)

PLAID JUBILEE Placement Diagram 44" x 20"

FIGURE 12 Center and fuse a circle in the center or each C-D unit and a star shape in the adjoining E units.

Step 3. Complete 20 A-B units, referring to **Figure 11** for placement of A-B units and to Step 6 of Piecing Blocks for instructions.

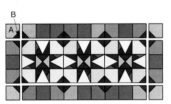

FIGURE 11 Complete 20 A-B units as shown for color placement of A-B units.

Step 4. Arrange the A-B units with A squares around the center again; stitch side units and squares to make strips. Press seams in one direction. Repeat for end strips.

Step 5. Sew side strips to the pieced block center; press seams away from center. Sew the end strips to opposite ends; press seams toward strips. Remove paper foundations.

Step 6. Trace circle and star shapes onto the paper side of the fusible web as directed on patterns for number to cut; cut out shapes leaving a margin around each one.

Step 7. Fuse shapes to the wrong side of fabrics as directed on patterns for color; cut out shapes on traced lines. Remove paper backing.

Step 8. Fuse a circle to the center of each C-D unit and each B section; center and fuse a star shape in the adjoining E units as shown in **Figure 12**.

Step 9. Cut (13) 4" x 4" squares fabric stabilizer; pin a square behind each fused shape.

Step 10. Using black all-purpose thread, machine buttonhole stitch around each fused shape to hold in place. Remove fabric stabilizer to complete the top.

Finishing the Quilt

Step 1. Sandwich the batting between the completed top and prepared backing piece; pin or baste to hold.

Step 2. Hand- or machine-quilt as desired.

Step 3. Trim batting and backing even with the quilted top.

Step 4. Join the binding strips on short ends with a diagonal seam to make a long strip; press seams toward one side.

Step 5. Press the strip in half along length with wrong sides together to complete the binding strip. Bind edges of quilt to finish. ◆

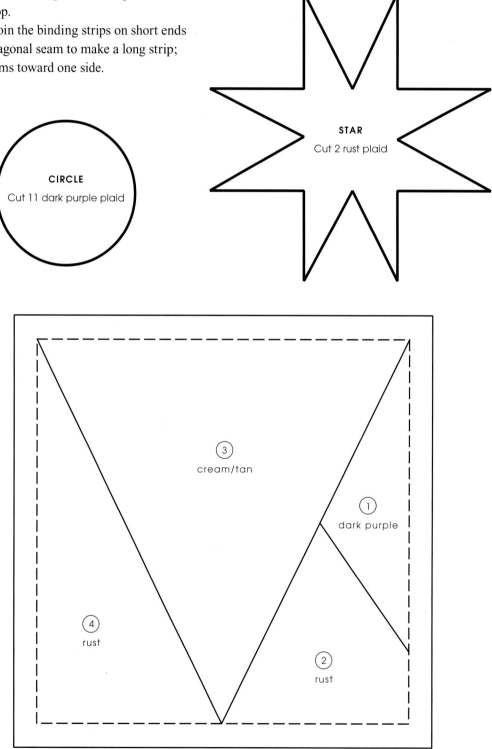

STAR
Cut 2 rust plaid

CIRCLE
Cut 11 dark purple plaid

③ cream/tan

① dark purple

④ rust

② rust

E FOUNDATION
Make 12 photocopies

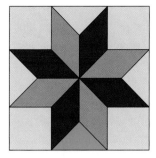

EIGHT-POINTED STAR
7½" x 7½" Block

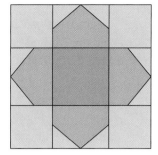

ORANGE FLOWER
7½" x 7½" Block

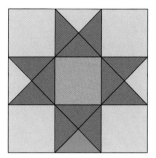

TRIANGLE FLOWER
7½" x 7½" Block

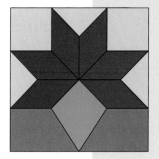

STAR FLOWER
7½" x 7½" Block

Flower Garden
Square

DESIGN > MARIAN SHENK

Create a grid of squares for the background of the pieced flowers.

PROJECT SPECIFICATIONS

Skill Level: Intermediate
Quilt Size: 41" x 36"
Block Size: 7½" x 7½"
Number of Blocks: 4

MATERIALS

- Scraps red, orchid, purple, pink, mauve, salmon and orange fabrics for flowers
- ¼ yard gold print
- ⅜ yard brown tonal
- ½ yard olive green mottled
- ⅝ yard bright green mottled
- ¾ yard blue mottled
- Backing 47" x 42"
- Batting 47" x 42"
- Neutral color all-purpose thread
- Quilting thread
- 2 packages brown wide bias tape
- Basic sewing tools and supplies

INSTRUCTIONS

Making Star Flower Block

Step 1. Prepare templates for all pieces using patterns given; cut as directed on each piece.

Step 2. Cut (10) 2¾" x 2¾" D squares blue mottled.

Step 3. Cut one square bright green mottled and two squares blue mottled 4¼" x 4¼"; cut each square on both diagonals to make A triangles. Discard three bright green triangles.

Step 4. Sew a red B to a red BR; press seams toward BR. Set in D between the B points as shown in **Figure 1**; repeat for two B-D units.

FIGURE 1 Join 2 B units and

set in D.

Step 5. Join the B-D units as shown in **Figure 2**; press.

FIGURE 2 Join the B-D units.

Step 6. Sew an E and ER to C and add a red B and BR as shown in **Figure 3**; press.

FIGURE 3 Sew E and ER

to C and add B and BR.

Step 7. Join the B-D unit with the B-C-E unit; set in blue A triangles to complete the Star Flower block as shown in **Figure 4**; press.

FIGURE 4 Join the pieced units

and set in A to complete the

Star Flower block.

Step 8. Set aside remaining pieces for other blocks.

Making Triangle Flower Block

Step 1. Cut one square each bright green and blue mottleds and three squares pink scrap 3¾" x 3¾"; cut each square in half on both

diagonals to make J triangles. Discard one blue and three bright green triangles.

Step 2. Cut one square mauve scrap and four squares blue mottled 3" x 3" for I.

Step 3. Join one blue and three pink J triangles as shown in **Figure 5**; repeat for three blue J units. Repeat with one bright green and three pink J triangles to make a green J unit, again referring to **Figure 5**.

FIGURE 5 Join J triangles

to make J units.

Step 4. Sew a blue J unit to opposite sides of the mauve I to make a row as shown in **Figure 6**; press seams toward I.

FIGURE 6 Join the pieced rows to

complete the Triangle Flower block.

Step 5. Sew a blue I to opposite pink sides of the remaining J units, again referring to **Figure 6**; press seams toward I.

Step 6. Join the pieced rows to complete the Triangle Flower block, again referring to **Figure 6**.

Making Orange Flower Block

Step 1. Cut one 3½" x 3½" F square from salmon scrap.

Step 2. Sew H and HR to G; press seams toward H and HR. Repeat for four units.

Step 3. Sew D to opposite sides of two G-H units as shown in **Figure 7**; press seams toward D. Repeat for two D-G-H rows.

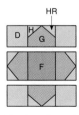

FIGURE 7 Join the pieced rows to

complete the Orange Flower block.

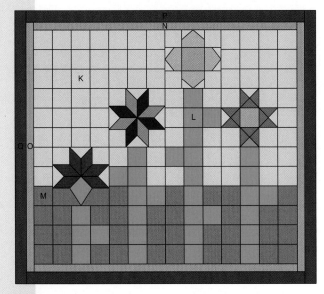

FLOWER GARDEN SQUARE Placement Diagram 41" x 36"

Making Eight-Pointed Star Block
Step 1. Join orchid B and purple BR pieces and set in D as for Star Flower block in **Figure 1**; press. Repeat for four B-D units.
Step 2. Join two B-D units as shown in **Figure 8**; press. Repeat for two B-D units.

FIGURE 8 Join B-D units and set in A to complete the Eight-Pointed Star block.

Step 3. Set in A triangles to complete the Eight-Pointed Star block, again referring to **Figure 8**.

Step 4. Sew a G-H unit to opposite sides of F, again referring to **Figure 7**; press seams toward F.
Step 5. Join the pieced rows to complete the Orange Flower block, again referring to **Figure 7**.

Completing the Top
Step 1. Cut 31 bright green mottled (L), 34 olive green mottled (M) and 67 blue mottled (K) 3" x 3" squares.

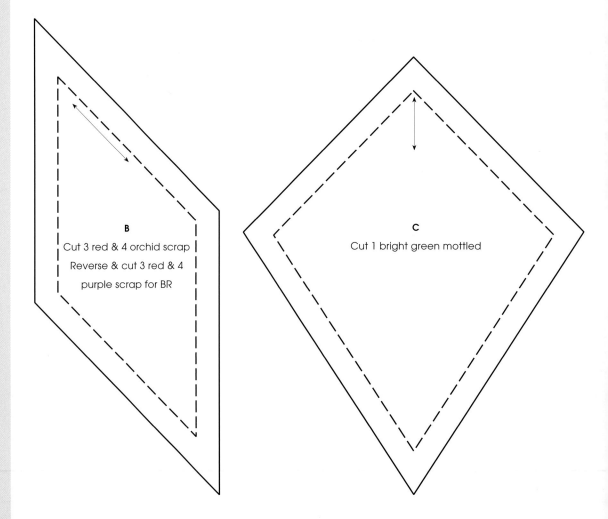

B
Cut 3 red & 4 orchid scrap
Reverse & cut 3 red & 4
purple scrap for BR

C
Cut 1 bright green mottled

Step 2. Arrange the K, L and M squares with the pieced blocks on a flat surface referring to the Placement Diagram. Join to complete the pieced center; press.

Step 3. Cut two 1½" x 35½" N strips and two 1½" x 32½" O strips gold print. Sew N strips to the top and bottom and O strips to opposite sides of the pieced center; press seams toward strips.

Step 4. Cut two 2½" x 37½" P strips and two 2½" x 36½" Q strips brown tonal. Sew P strips to the top and bottom and Q strips to opposite sides of the pieced center; press seams toward strips.

Finishing the Quilt

Step 1. Sandwich the batting between the completed top and prepared backing; pin or baste layers together to hold.

Step 2. Hand- or machine-quilt as desired. When quilting is complete, trim batting and backing even with top; remove pins or basting.

Step 3. Bind edges with brown wide bias tape to finish. ◆

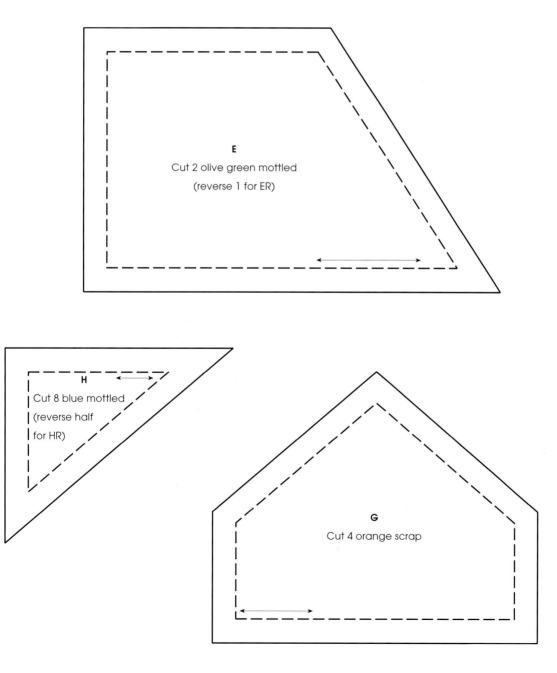

E
Cut 2 olive green mottled
(reverse 1 for ER)

H
Cut 8 blue mottled
(reverse half
for HR)

G
Cut 4 orange scrap

FOUR-STRIPE
7½" x 7½" Block

LILY
7½" x 7½" Block

Bed of Lilies

DESIGN > MARIAN SHENK

Pieced lily blocks are stitched to make a wide table runner.

PROJECT SPECIFICATIONS

Skill Level: Beginner
Runner Size: 44½" x 23¼"
Block Size: 7½" x 7½"
Number of Blocks: 11

MATERIALS

- 1 fat quarter each medium and dark green tonals
- ¼ yard white tonal
- ⅜ each pink and rose tonals
- ½ yard each burgundy floral and burgundy tonal
- Backing 50" x 29"
- Batting 50" x 29"
- Neutral color all-purpose thread
- Quilting thread
- Basic sewing tools and supplies

INSTRUCTIONS

Cutting

Step 1. Prepare templates using pattern pieces given; cut as directed on each piece.

Step 2. Cut two 6¼" x 6¼" squares burgundy floral; cut each square on one diagonal to make (4) G triangles.

Step 3. Cut two 11⅞" x 11⅞" squares burgundy floral; cut each square in half on both diagonals to make (8) H triangles.

Step 4. Cut (and piece) two 1½" x 23¾" I strips and two 1½" x 43" J strips rose tonal.

Step 5. Cut four 2¼" by fabric width strips burgundy tonal for binding.

Piecing Lily Blocks

Step 1. To piece one Lily block, sew a pink A to a rose AR; press seam toward AR. Repeat with a rose A and a pink AR.

Step 2. Referring to **Figure 1**, join the A-AR units and set in C and white B pieces. Press seams toward B and away from C. Add dark green D; press seam toward D.

FIGURE 1 Join pieces as shown to complete 1 unit.

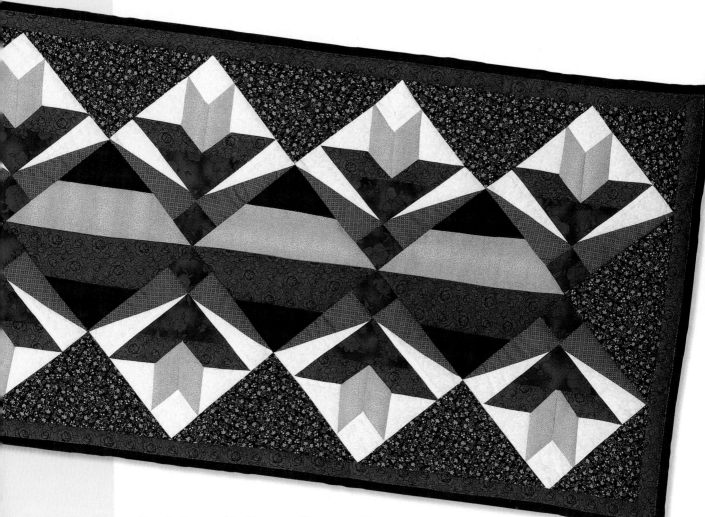

Step 3. Sew a white E to a medium green E; press seam toward darker fabric. Repeat to make an ER unit.

Step 4. Sew an E unit to the A-B-C-D unit; press seams toward E.

Step 5. Referring to **Figure 2**, sew a dark green B to one end of the ER unit; sew the B-ER unit to the pieced unit to complete one Lily block. Press seams toward B-ER. Repeat for eight blocks.

FIGURE 2 Join units to complete 1 Lily block.

Piecing Four Stripe Blocks

Step 1. Sew a burgundy D to a pink F and a burgundy D to a rose F as shown in **Figure 3**; press seams toward D.

FIGURE 3 Sew D to F.

Step 2. Join the D-F units to complete one Four-Stripe block as shown in **Figure 4**; press seam in one direction. Repeat for three blocks.

FIGURE 4 Join the units to complete 1 Four Stripe block.

Completing the Top

Step 1. Arrange the pieced blocks with the G and H triangles as shown in **Figure 5**; join to make rows. Press seams toward G and H.

FIGURE 5 Arrange blocks with G and H pieces.

Step 2. Sew a J strip to opposite long sides and I strips to opposite short ends of the pieced center; press seams toward strips to complete the pieced top.

Finishing the Quilt
Step 1. Sandwich the batting between the completed top and prepared backing; pin or baste layers together to hold.

Step 2. Hand- or machine-quilt as desired. When quilting is complete, trim batting and backing even with top; remove pins or basting.

Step 3. Join the previously cut binding strips on short ends to make one long strip. Fold the strip in half along length with wrong sides together; press.

Step 4. Sew binding to quilt edges, mitering corners and overlapping ends. Fold binding to the backside and stitch in place. ◆

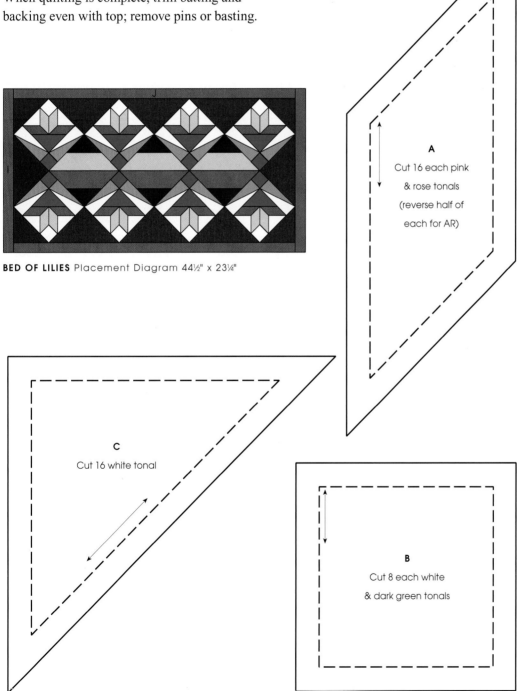

BED OF LILIES Placement Diagram 44½" x 23¼"

A
Cut 16 each pink
& rose tonals
(reverse half of
each for AR)

C
Cut 16 white tonal

B
Cut 8 each white
& dark green tonals

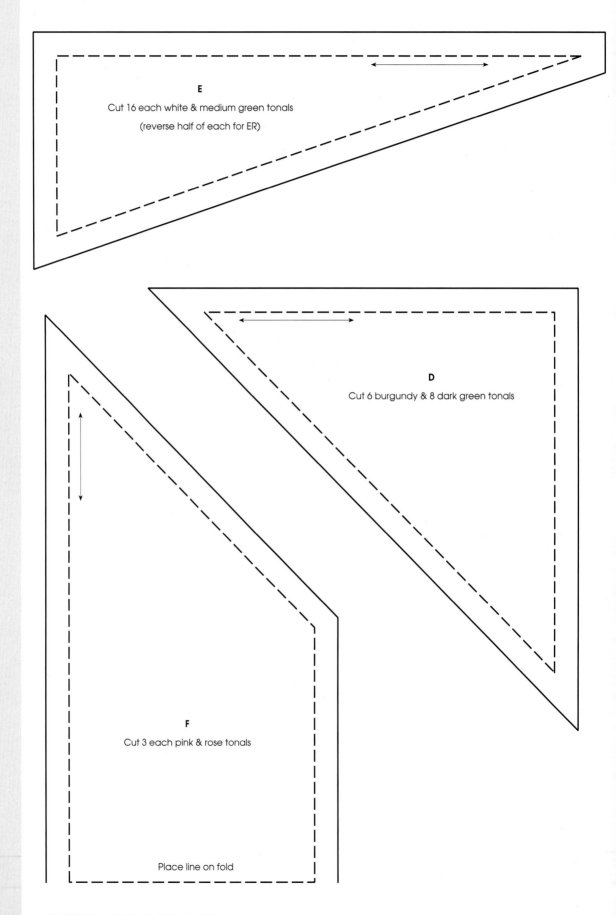

E

Cut 16 each white & medium green tonals

(reverse half of each for ER)

D

Cut 6 burgundy & 8 dark green tonals

F

Cut 3 each pink & rose tonals

Place line on fold

Denim Table Runner

DESIGN > CONNIE KAUFFMAN

Use up lots of denim scraps from your old jeans in

this small table runner.

PROJECT SPECIFICATIONS

Skill Level: Intermediate

Quilt Size: 26" x 14"

MATERIALS

- 7" x 7" square denim for center
- ¼ yard total denim scraps
- ¼ yard total indigo print scraps
- Backing 32" x 20"
- Batting 32" x 20"
- Matching all-purpose thread
- Quilting thread
- Basic tools and supplies

INSTRUCTIONS

Step 1. Prepare templates using pattern pieces given; cut as directed on each piece.

Step 2. Lay out the pieces on a flat surface and stitch together aligning one end of each piece to make a straight edge in the following order referring to **Figure 1**: A denim, B indigo, C denim, D indigo, D denim, D indigo, E denim, E indigo and E denim. Press seams in one direction. Repeat for two units.

FIGURE 1 Lay out pieces as shown.

Step 3. Repeat with the remaining pieces in the following order, again referring to **Figure 1**: A indigo, B denim, C indigo, DR denim, DR indigo, DR denim, ER indigo, ER denim and ER indigo. Press seams in opposite direction from previously pieced units. Repeat for two units.

Step 4. Join two units as shown in **Figure 2**, stopping stitching ¼" from the inside edge as shown in **Figure 3**; press seam open. Repeat with remaining two units.

FIGURE 2 Join 2 units.

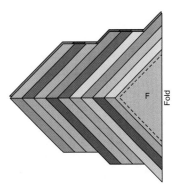

FIGURE 5 Fold the pieced unit
down the center of F.

FIGURE 3 Stop stitching ¼"
from inside edge.

Step 5. Sew one side of the F square to the inside edge of one pieced unit, beginning and ending stitching at the ¼" seam as shown in **Figure 4**; stop and cut thread. Turn the piece and sew the adjacent side of the F square to the adjacent edge of the pieced unit in the same manner. Press seam away from F.

FIGURE 6 Stitch the edge
seams from F to the outside.

Step 8. Lay the batting piece on a flat surface with the backing piece right side up. Pin the completed runner top right sides together with the backing.

Step 9. Sew all around the outside edge, leaving a 4" opening along one end; trim batting and backing even with runner top, clip corners and inside corner seams and turn right side out through opening.

Step 10. Turn edge of opening to the inside; press the entire top flat. Hand-stitch the opening closed.

Step 11. Machine-quilt in the ditch of seams and in the center of F using a fancy quilting design to finish. ◆

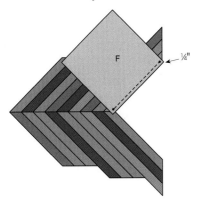

FIGURE 4 Sew F to the inside edge
of 1 unit beginning and ending
stitching at the ¼" seam.

Step 6. Sew the remaining pieced unit to the F square in the same manner; press seams away from F.

Step 7. Fold the pieced unit right sides together down the center of F as shown in **Figure 5**; stitch the edge seams from F to the outside as shown in **Figure 6**. Press seams open.

DENIM TABLE RUNNER Placement Diagram 26" x 14"

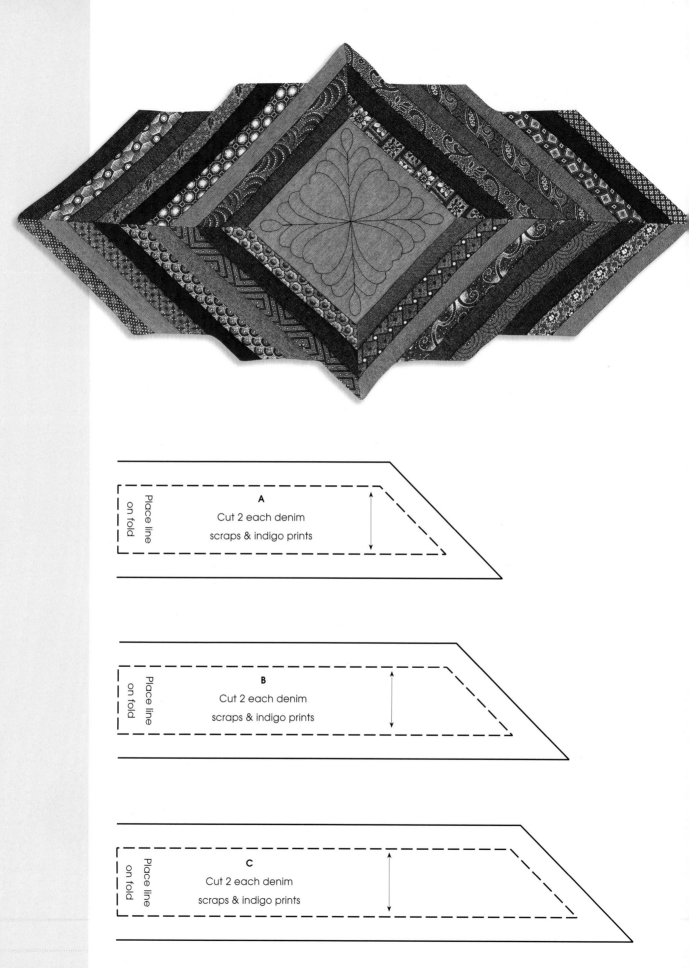

A

Place line on fold

Cut 2 each denim scraps & indigo prints

B

Place line on fold

Cut 2 each denim scraps & indigo prints

C

Place line on fold

Cut 2 each denim scraps & indigo prints

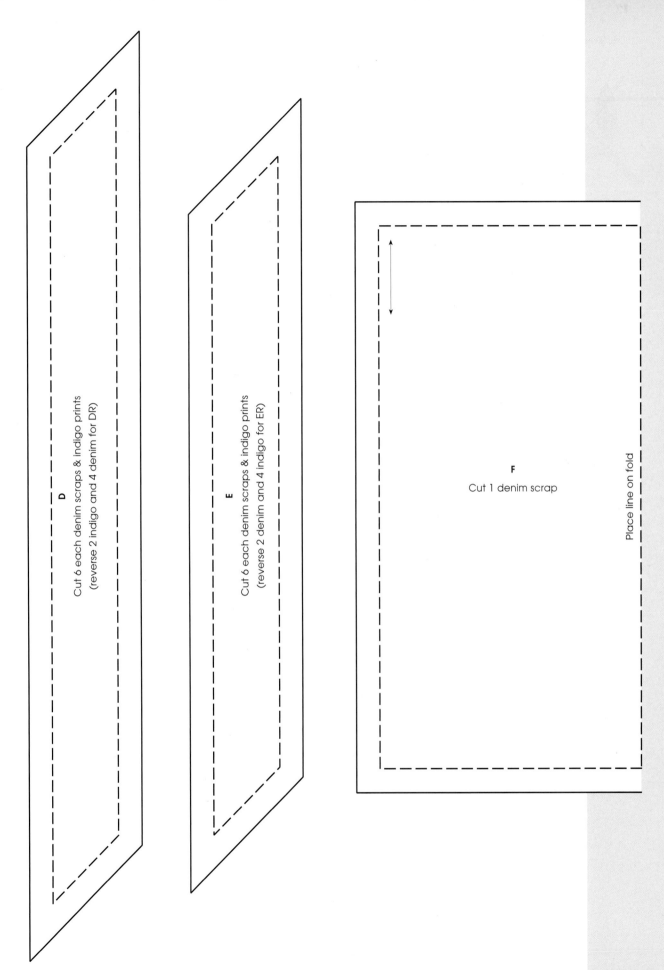

D

Cut 6 each denim scraps & indigo prints
(reverse 2 indigo and 4 denim for DR)

E

Cut 6 each denim scraps & indigo prints
(reverse 2 denim and 4 indigo for ER)

F

Cut 1 denim scrap

Place line on fold

TULIP
9" x 9" Block

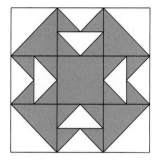

CROSSED T's
9" x 9" Block

T Is for Tulips

DESIGN > BETTY ALDERMAN

The Crossed T's blocks combine with appliquéd tulip blocks to make a pretty quilt with an antique look.

PROJECT SPECIFICATIONS
Skill Level: Intermediate
Quilt Size: 47¼" x 47¼"
Block Size: 9" x 9" and 4½" x 4½"
Number of Blocks: 13 and 4

MATERIALS
- ¼ yard each 9 different dark prints for Crossed T's blocks
- ¼ yard pink print for tulip appliqué
- ¼ yard pink print for inner border
- ½ yard binding fabric
- ⅝ yard white shirting print for A and B background squares
- ⅝ yard blue print for outer border
- ¾ yard total of 1 or more white shirting prints for Crossed T's blocks
- ¾ yard total of 1 or more dark brown prints for H and I triangles
- Backing 53" x 53"
- Batting 53" x 53"
- Neutral color all-purpose thread
- Machine-appliqué thread to match pink and brown prints
- Quilting thread
- 1 yard lightweight fusible web
- ⅝ yard fabric stabilizer
- Basic sewing tools and supplies

INSTRUCTIONS
Making Large & Small Tulip Blocks
Step 1. Prepare templates for appliqué shapes using patterns given.

Step 2. Trace shapes onto the paper side of the lightweight fusible web referring to patterns for number to cut. Cut out shapes, leaving a margin around each one.

Step 3. Fuse paper shapes to the wrong side of fabrics as directed on pieces for color; cut out shapes on traced lines. Remove paper backing.

Step 4. Cut four 9½" x 9½" A and four 5" x 5" B squares white shirting fabric. Fold and crease to mark the diagonal center.

Step 5. Center one large stem shape on the diagonal of each A square as shown in **Figure 1**; fuse in place. Repeat with small stems and B squares.

FIGURE 1 Center 1 large stem
shape on the diagonal of A.

Step 6. Arrange two large leaves and one large tulip shape with the fused stem shape on each A square; fuse in place. Repeat with small leaves and small tulip shapes on B.

Step 7. Cut four 9½" x 9½" and four 5" x 5" squares fabric stabilizer; pin squares behind same-size fused squares.

Step 8. Using machine-appliqué thread to match fabrics, satin-stitch shapes in place. When stitching is complete, remove fabric stabilizer to complete the blocks.

Making Crossed T's Blocks

Step 1. To make one Crossed T's block, cut (16) 2" x 2" C squares, one 3½" x 3½" D square and two 3⅞" x 3⅞" E squares from one of the nine dark prints. Cut each E square in half on one diagonal to make E triangles.

Step 2. Cut eight 2" x 3½" F rectangles and two 3⅞" x 3⅞" G squares from white shirting print. Cut each G square in half on one diagonal to make G triangles.

Step 3. Mark a diagonal line on the wrong side of each C square. Referring to **Figure 2**, pin C to F and stitch on the marked line; trim seam to ¼" and press C to the right side. Repeat on opposite end of F to complete one C-F unit, again referring to **Figure 2**; repeat for eight units.

FIGURE 2 Complete 1 C-F unit.

Step 4. Sew E to G to make an E-G unit as shown in **Figure 3**; press seam toward E. Repeat for four units.

FIGURE 3 Make an E-G unit.

Step 5. To complete one block, join two C-F units as shown in **Figure 4**; repeat for four joined units.

FIGURE 4 Join 2 C-F units.

Step 6. Join two E-G units with a joined C-F unit to make a row as shown in **Figure 5**; repeat for two rows. Press seams toward E-G units.

FIGURE 5 Join units to make
a row.

Step 7. Join D with two joined C-F units to make a row as shown in **Figure 6**; press seams toward D.

FIGURE 6 Join units with D to
make a row.

Step 8. Join the rows to complete one Crossed T's block referring to **Figure 7**; press. Repeat for nine blocks.

FIGURE 7 Join the rows to complete
1 Crossed T's block.

Completing the Top

Step 1. Cut two 14" x 14" squares dark brown print; cut each square in half on both diagonals to make H triangles.

Step 2. Cut two 7¼" x 7¼" squares dark brown print; cut each square in half on one diagonal to make I triangles.

Step 3. Arrange the blocks in diagonal rows with H and I triangles as shown in **Figure 8**. Join in rows; join rows to complete the quilt center. Press seams in one direction.

FIGURE 8 Arrange the blocks in
diagonal rows with H and I
triangles.

Step 4. Cut four 1½" x 36¾" J strips pink print and four 4" x 36¾" K strips blue print. Cut eight 1½" x 5" L strips pink print.

Step 5. Sew a J strip to a K strip with right sides together along length; press seams toward K. Sew L to each end as shown in **Figure 9**; press seams toward L. Repeat for four J-K-L strips.

FIGURE 9 Sew L to each end of a J-K strip.

Step 6. Sew a J-K-L strip to opposite sides of the pieced center; press seams toward strips.

Step 7. Sew a Small Tulip block to each end of the remaining J-K-L strips, keeping blocks upright on each end; press seams away from blocks. Sew these strips to the top and bottom of the quilt center; press seams toward strips.

Finishing the Quilt

Step 1. Sandwich the batting between the completed top and prepared backing; pin or baste layers together to hold.

Step 2. Hand- or machine-quilt as desired. When quilting is complete, trim batting and backing even with top; remove pins or basting.

T IS FOR TULIPS Placement Diagram 47¼" x 47¼"

Step 3. Cut five 2¼" by fabric width strips binding fabric. Join the strips on short ends to make one long strip. Fold the strip in half along length with wrong sides together; press.

Step 4. Sew binding to quilt edges, mitering corners and overlapping ends. Fold binding to the backside and stitch in place. ◆

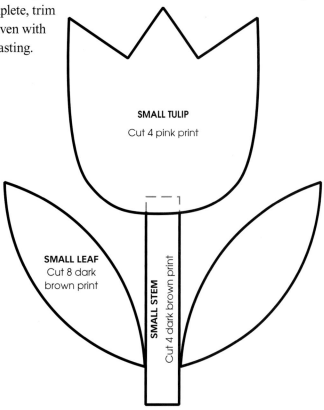

SMALL TULIP
Cut 4 pink print

SMALL LEAF
Cut 8 dark
brown print

SMALL STEM
Cut 4 dark brown print

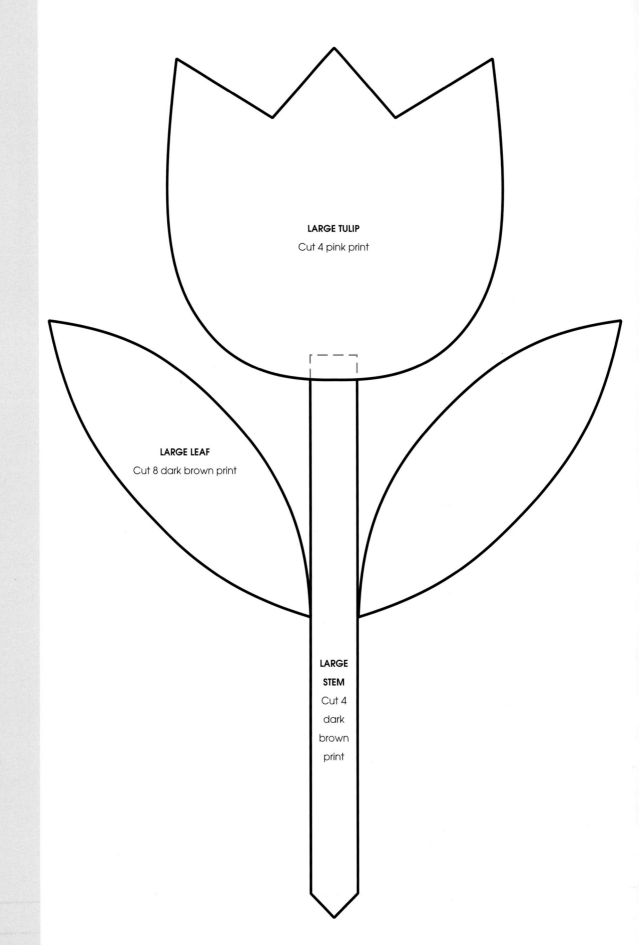

LARGE TULIP

Cut 4 pink print

LARGE LEAF

Cut 8 dark brown print

LARGE STEM

Cut 4 dark brown print

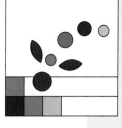

JINGLEBERRIES
13½" x 13½" Block

Crazy About
Jingleberries

DESIGN > RHONDA TAYLOR

Crazy-patchwork borders frame the center appliqué design

on this holiday table cover or wall quilt.

PROJECT SPECIFICATIONS

Skill Level: Beginner
Quilt Size: 36" x 36"
Block Size: 13½" x 13½"
Number of Blocks: 4

MATERIALS

- Scraps red, blue, medium and dark green,
  gold and cream prints, plaids or checks
- ¼ yard cream print
- ⅓ yard gold plaid for binding
- ¾ yard cream-with-red dot
- Backing 42" x 42"
- Batting 42" x 42"
- Neutral color and black all-purpose thread
- Quilting thread
- Red 6-strand embroidery floss
- ⅔ yard lightweight interfacing
  for foundations
- ¼ yard fusible web
- ¾ yard fabric stabilizer
- Basic sewing tools and supplies

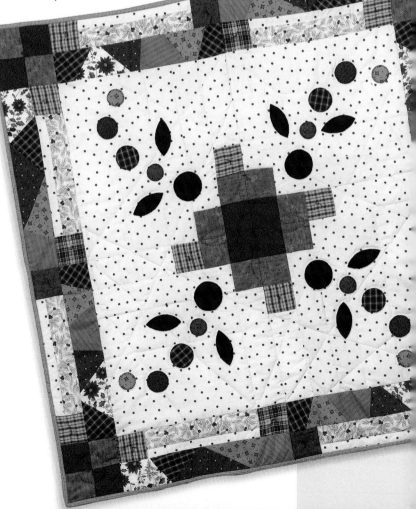

INSTRUCTIONS

Cutting

Step 1. Cut four 9½" x 14" A rectangles from cream-with-red dot.

Step 2. Cut the following 2¾" x 2¾" squares: 12 gold (B), 20 medium green (C), four red plaid (D) and 12 red print (E).

Step 3. Cut four 2¾" x 11¾" (F) strips and four 2¾" x 7¼" (G) strips cream-with-red dot.

Step 4. Cut eight 2" x 9½" H strips cream print and eight 1¼" x 9½" I strips cream-with-red dot.

Step 5. Trace four copies each J and K foundation patterns onto the lightweight interfacing.

Step 6. Cut fabric scraps in colors indicated on patterns for crazy patchwork piecing, cutting pieces at least ¼" larger than pattern space all around. Note that the same fabric is used in the same number location on each J and K piece.

Step 7. Prepare templates for appliqué pieces; trace shapes onto the paper side of the fusible web as directed on shapes for number to cut. Cut out shapes, leaving a margin around each one. Fuse shapes to the wrong side of fabric scraps as directed on each piece for color. Cut out shapes on traced lines; remove paper.

Completing the Blocks

Step 1. Sew a C square to F; press seam toward C.

Step 2. Sew an E square to a C square to a B square and add to G as shown in **Figure 1**; press seams away from G.

FIGURE 1 Sew an E square to a C square to a B square and add to G.

Step 3. Sew the C-F strip to A and add the B-C-E-G strip as shown in **Figure 2**; press seams toward A.

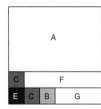

FIGURE 2 Sew the C-F strip to A and add the B-C-E-G strip.

Step 4. Transfer appliqué placement to the A and F rectangles using full-size pattern placement.

Step 5. Arrange shapes on A and F and fuse in place referring to the block drawing.

Step 6. Cut a 10" x 12" rectangle fabric stabilizer; pin behind fused shapes. Machine blanket-stitch around each shape using black all-purpose thread to complete one Jingleberries block; repeat for four blocks. Remove fabric stabilizer.

Completing the Top

Step 1. Join two blocks to make a row as shown in **Figure 3**; repeat for two rows. Press seams in alternating directions. Join the rows to complete the pieced center referring to the Placement Diagram for positioning of rows.

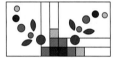

FIGURE 3 Join 2 blocks to make a row.

Step 2. Sew H to I; press seams toward H; repeat for eight H-I units.

Step 3. Add C to one end and B to the other end of an H-I unit as shown in **Figure 4**; press seams toward C and B. Repeat for four C-B-H-I units.

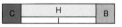

FIGURE 4 Add C to 1 end and B to the other end of an H-I unit.

Step 4. Add B to one end and D to the other end of an H-I unit as shown in **Figure 5**; press seams toward B and D. Repeat for four B-D-H-I units.

FIGURE 5 Add B to 1 end and D to the other end of an H-I unit.

Step 5. Referring to **Figure 6**, place piece 1 on the unmarked side of a J foundation strip; place piece 2 right sides together with piece 1. Turn to the marked side and stitch on the line between pieces 1 and 2; trim seam to ¼". Turn over and press piece 2 to the right side. Continue adding pieces in numerical order by color referring to

the patterns. Repeat to make four each J and K crazy-patchwork strips. Trim fabric even with outer line on foundations.

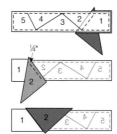

FIGURE 6 Sew piece 2 to piece 1 on the unmarked side; turn to the right side, trim seam and press piece 2 to the right side.

Step 6. Sew K to the H side of each B-C-H-I unit as shown in **Figure 7**; press seam away from K.

FIGURE 7 Sew K to the H side of each B-C-H-I unit.

Step 7. Sew J to the I side of each B-D-H-I unit as shown in **Figure 8**; press seam away from J.

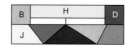

FIGURE 8 Sew J to the I side of each B-D-H-I unit.

Step 8. Join one B-D-H-I-J unit and one B-C-H-I-K as shown in **Figure 9**; repeat for four units. Sew a unit to opposite sides of the pieced center as shown in **Figure 10**. Press seams toward A.

FIGURE 9 Join 1 B-D-H-I-J unit and 1 B-C-H-I-K.

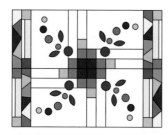

FIGURE 10 Sew a unit to opposite sides of the pieced center.

Step 9. Sew a C square to an E square; press seams toward C. Repeat for eight C-E units. Join two C-E units to complete a corner unit as shown in **Figure 11**; repeat for four corner units. Press seams in one direction.

FIGURE 11 Join 2 C-E units to complete a corner unit.

Step 10. Sew a corner unit to each end of the remaining pieced strips as shown in **Figure 12**; press seams toward corner units. Sew these strips to the pieced center referring to the Placement Diagram for positioning; press seams toward A.

FIGURE 12 Sew a corner unit to each end of the remaining pieced strips.

Finishing the Quilt

Step 1. Sandwich the batting between the completed top and prepared backing; pin or baste layers together to hold.

Step 2. Quilt or tie as desired. When quilting is complete, trim batting and backing even with top; remove pins or basting.

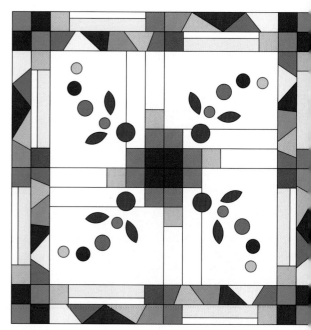

CRAZY ABOUT JINGLEBERRIES Placement Diagram 36" x 36"

Step 3. Cut four 2¼" by fabric width strips gold plaid for binding. Join strips on short ends to make one long strip. Fold the strip in half along length with wrong sides together; press.

Step 4. Sew binding to quilt edges, mitering corners and overlapping ends. Fold binding to the backside and stitch in place to finish. ◆

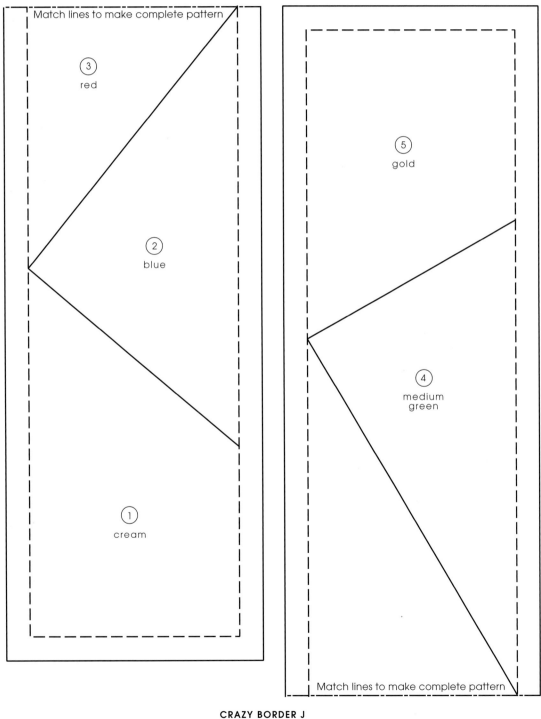

CRAZY BORDER J

Make 4

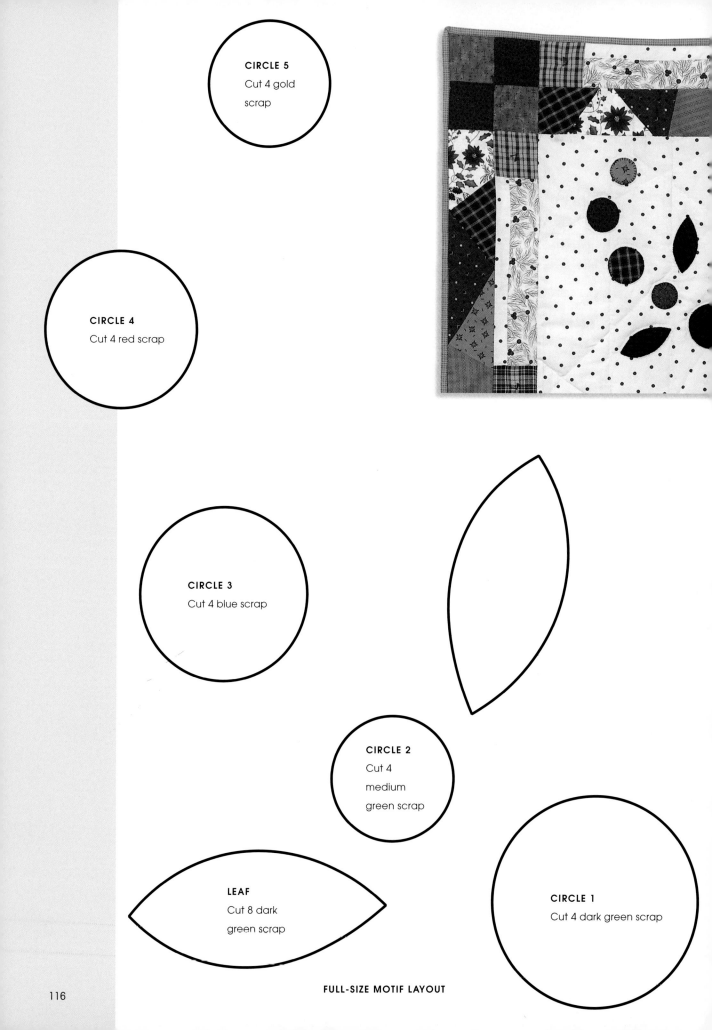

CIRCLE 5
Cut 4 gold
scrap

CIRCLE 4
Cut 4 red scrap

CIRCLE 3
Cut 4 blue scrap

CIRCLE 2
Cut 4
medium
green scrap

LEAF
Cut 8 dark
green scrap

CIRCLE 1
Cut 4 dark green scrap

FULL-SIZE MOTIF LAYOUT

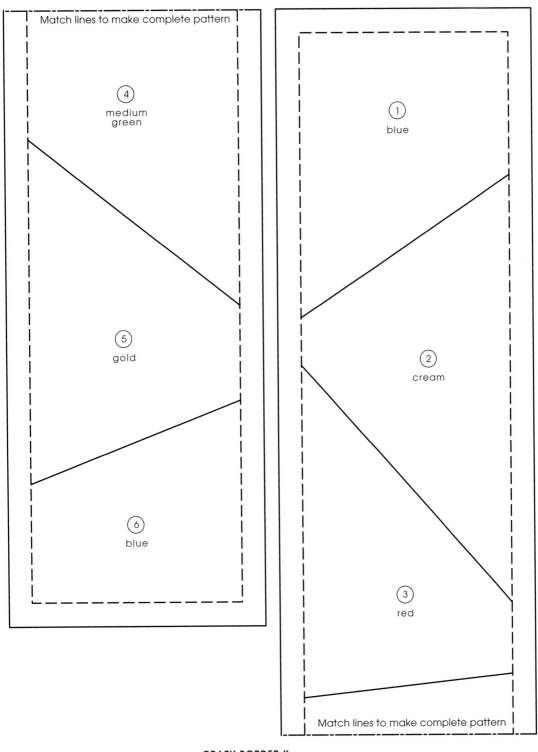

Match lines to make complete pattern

④ medium green

⑤ gold

⑥ blue

① blue

② cream

③ red

Match lines to make complete pattern

CRAZY BORDER K

Make 4

FLOATING TRIANGLES

12" x 12" Block

Floating Triangles
Wall Quilt

DESIGN > PAT CAMPBELL

Try a four-block wall quilt featuring a different color in each block.

PROJECT NOTES

Select light and dark scraps of four different colors. The sample uses blue, green, brown and red. Solids, tonals, prints, stripes, dots and plaids all work. Be sure there is a contrast between the lights and darks to make the design appear.

PROJECT SPECIFICATIONS

Skill Level: Beginner
Quilt Size: 27" x 27"
Block Size: 12" x 12"
Number of Blocks: 4

MATERIALS

- Assorted lights and darks of 4 different color families
- 2 light strips 2" x 12½" from each color family for D
- 1 dark square 2" x 2" from each color family for E
- ⅜ yard binding fabric
- Backing 33" x 33"

- Batting 33" x 33"
- Neutral color all-purpose thread
- Quilting thread
- Basic sewing tools and supplies

INSTRUCTIONS

Piecing the Blocks

Step 1. Copy foundation patterns for A, B and C units as directed on each foundation piece.

Step 2. Cut fabric patches for foundations as directed on patterns for color (light or dark), being sure that pieces are at least ¼" larger than each required piece. ***Note:*** *Keep fabric patches of darks and lights in each color family together for stitching. For example, keep all light green patches together for the green blocks.*

Step 3. Referring to the order of piecing and light and dark color placement on the A unit foundation and to **Figure 1**, pin piece 2 to piece 1 on the unmarked side of the foundation pattern; turn paper over and stitch on the line between pieces 1 and 2. Press piece 2 to the right side; trim excess beyond seams as

needed. Continue adding pieces in numerical order, pressing each added piece to the right side after stitching. Repeat for all A, B and C foundation units.

Step 4. When all foundation units have been stitched, trim edges even with paper foundation patterns as shown in **Figure 2**.

FIGURE 1 Stitch piece 2 to piece 1.

FIGURE 2 Trim fabric edges even with foundation pattern.

FLOATING TRIANGLES WALL QUILT Placement Diagram 27" x 27"

Step 7. Sew a C unit to each side of the A-B units to complete one block as shown in **Figure 5**; repeat for four different-color blocks.

FIGURE 5 Sew a C unit to each side of the A-B units to complete 1 block.

Step 8. Arrange the blocks in two rows of two blocks each; join blocks to make rows. Press seams open. Join rows to complete the pieced center; press seams open.

Step 9. Join two D strips on short ends referring to the Placement Diagram for positioning of colors; press seams open. Repeat for four D units.

Step 10. Sew a D unit to opposite sides of the pieced center; press seams toward D units.

Step 11. Sew an E square to each end of the remaining D units, again referring to the Placement Diagram for positioning of colors; press seams toward D.

Step 12. Sew a D-E strip to the top and bottom of the pieced center; press seams toward D-E strips.

Step 5. To complete one block, join three A units of one color family as shown in **Figure 3**; press seams open.

FIGURE 3 Join 3 A units of 1 color family.

FIGURE 4 Sew a B unit to each side of an A unit.

Step 6. Sew a B unit to each side of an A unit as shown in **Figure 4**; press seams toward B units.

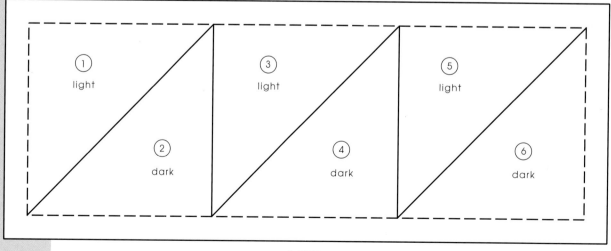

A UNIT

Make 12 copies

Stitch 3 of each color family

Finishing the Quilt

Step 1. Sandwich the batting between the completed top and prepared backing; pin or baste layers together to hold.

Step 2. Hand- or machine-quilt as desired. When quilting is complete, trim batting and backing even with top; remove pins or basting.

Step 3. Cut four 2¼" by fabric width strips binding fabric. Join strips on short ends to make one long strip. Fold the strip in half along length with wrong sides together; press.

Step 4. Sew binding to quilt edges, mitering corners and overlapping ends. Fold binding to the backside and stitch in place to finish. ◆

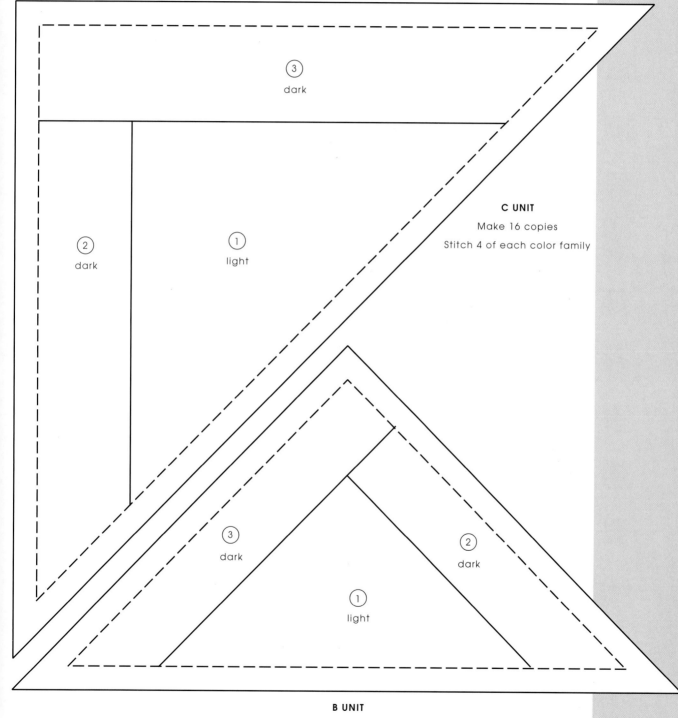

③ dark

② dark

① light

C UNIT
Make 16 copies
Stitch 4 of each color family

③ dark

② dark

① light

B UNIT
Make 16 copies
Stitch 4 of each color family

BATS
9" x 10" Block

PUMPKINS
9" x 10" Block

WITCH
9" x 12" Block

CAT
9" x 12" Block

Spooky
Halloween

DESIGN > BARBARA CLAYTON

Appliqué lends itself to the use of scraps in this

Halloween wall quilt.

PROJECT SPECIFICATIONS

Skill Level: Beginner
Quilt Size: 24" x 28"
Block Size: 9" x 10" and 9" x 12"
Number of Blocks: 4

MATERIALS

- Scraps white, orange, green, black, yellow, gold, peach and brown prints, solids or tonals
- ¼ yard white tonal
- ⅓ yard medium and dark purple tonals
- ⅓ yard green dot
- ⅓ yard blue tonal
- ½ yard black tonal
- ⅞ yard orange stripe
- Backing 30" x 34"
- Batting 30" x 34"
- Neutral color all-purpose thread
- Quilting thread
- ¾ yard no-sew fusible web
- Black fine-point permanent marker
- Basic sewing tools and supplies

INSTRUCTIONS

Cutting

Step 1. Prepare templates for appliqué shapes using full-size patterns given; trace shapes on the paper side of the no-sew fusible web. Cut out shapes, leaving a margin around each one. *Note: Patterns are given in reverse for fusible appliqué.*

Step 2. Fuse shapes to the wrong side of fabric scraps as directed on each piece for color; cut out shapes on traced lines. Remove paper backing.

Step 3. Cut a 9½" x 10½" rectangle from medium (A) and dark purple (B) tonals and a 9½" x 12½" rectangle from green dot (C) and blue tonal (D).

Step 4. Cut three 1½" by fabric width strips each black (E) and white (F) tonals.

Step 5. Cut 10 orange scrap (G) squares 1½" x 1½".

Step 6. Cut two 2" x 25½" H strips and two 2" x 24½" I strips along length of orange stripe.

Step 7. Cut one 2½" x 21" strip black tonal for J hanging loops.

Step 8. Cut three 2¼" by fabric width strips black tonal for binding.

Appliqué Blocks

Step 1. Fold and crease A, B, C and D rectangles to mark the centers.

Step 2. Using full-size patterns and center marks as guides, arrange and fuse shapes in numerical order on the appropriate backgrounds as indicated on patterns.

Step 3. Using the black fine-point permanent marker, add detail lines to pumpkins, broom, witch's eye and hair as marked on patterns.

Completing the Top

Step 1. Sew an E strip to an F strip with right sides together along length; press seams toward E. Repeat for three strip sets. Subcut strip sets into (62) 1½" E-F units as shown in **Figure 1**.

FIGURE 1 Subcut strip sets into 1½" E-F units.

Step 2. Join five E-F units to make a strip as shown in **Figure 2**; press seams in one direction. Repeat for 10 five-unit strips and two six-unit strips.

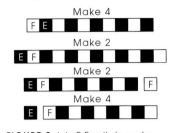

FIGURE 2 Join E-F units to make strips; remove squares as shown.

Step 3. Remove one E square from four five-unit strips and one F segment from two five-unit strips, again referring to **Figure 2**.

Step 4. Arrange the shortened five-unit strips with the completed blocks as shown in **Figure 3**; join to complete rows. Press seams away from strips.

FIGURE 3 Join shortened 5-unit strips with the completed blocks to make rows.

Step 5. Join one removed E square with four G squares and two five-unit strips to make a center strip as shown in **Figure 4**; press seams in one direction.

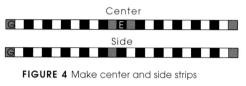

FIGURE 4 Make center and side strips as shown.

Step 6. Join one six-unit strip with one five-unit strip and three G squares to make a side strip again referring to **Figure 4**; repeat for two side strips. Press seams in one direction.

Step 7. Join the rows with the center and side strips referring to **Figure 5**; press seams away from strips.

FIGURE 5 Join the rows with the center and side strips.

Step 8. Sew the H strips to opposite sides and I strips to the top and bottom of the pieced center; press seams toward H and I.

Finishing the Quilt

Step 1. Sandwich the batting between the completed top and prepared backing; pin or baste layers together to hold.

Step 2. Hand- or machine-quilt as desired. *Note: The sample shown was hand-quilted ¼" away from appliqué motifs and machine-quilted in the ditch of pieced seams.* When quilting is complete, trim batting and backing even with top; remove pins or basting.

Step 3. Join the previously cut binding strips on short ends to make one long strip. Fold the strip in half along length with wrong sides together; press.

Step 4. Sew binding to quilt edges, mitering corners and overlapping ends. Fold binding to the backside and stitch in place.

SPOOKY HALLOWEEN Placement Diagram 24" x 28"

Step 5. Fold the J strip in half along length with right sides together; stitch to make a tube.

Step 6. Turn the J tube right side out; press flat. Cut into seven 3" J pieces.

Step 7. Pin a J piece with one raw edge even with top bound corner as shown in **Figure 6**; stitch in place along binding seam, again referring to **Figure 6**.

FIGURE 6 Pin a J piece with 1 raw edge even with top bound corner; stitch in place along binding seam.

Step 8. Flip the J piece to the backside to make a loop; turn under raw edge ¼". Hand-stitch in place to make a hanging loop.

Step 9. Repeat Steps 7 and 8 across the top of the quilt, spacing the J loops evenly along the top edge to finish. ◆

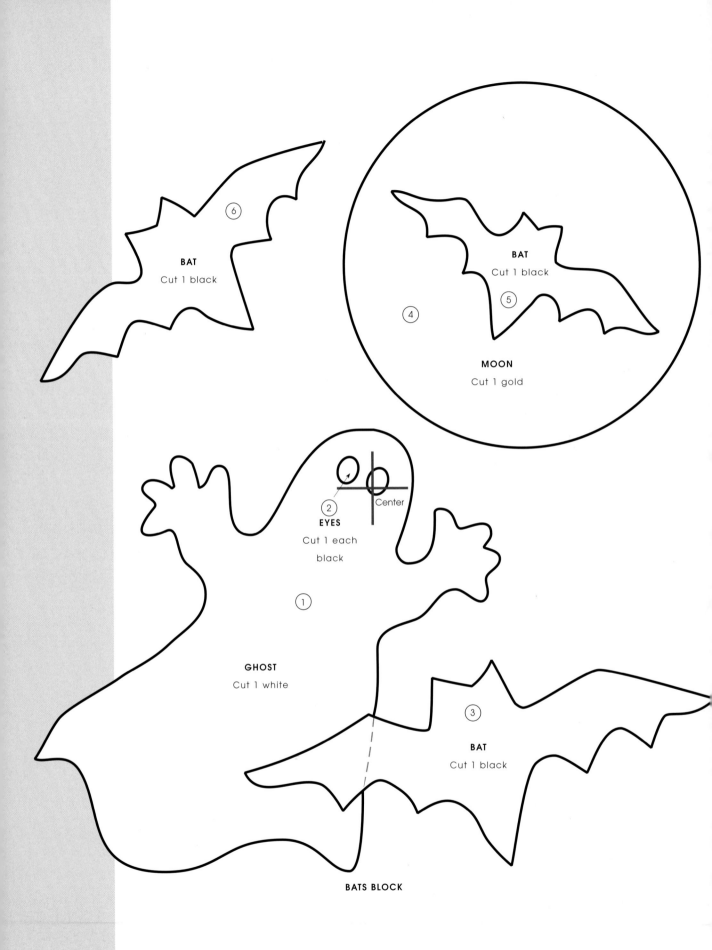

⑥

BAT

Cut 1 black

④

BAT

Cut 1 black

⑤

MOON

Cut 1 gold

②

Center

EYES

Cut 1 each
black

①

GHOST

Cut 1 white

③

BAT

Cut 1 black

BATS BLOCK

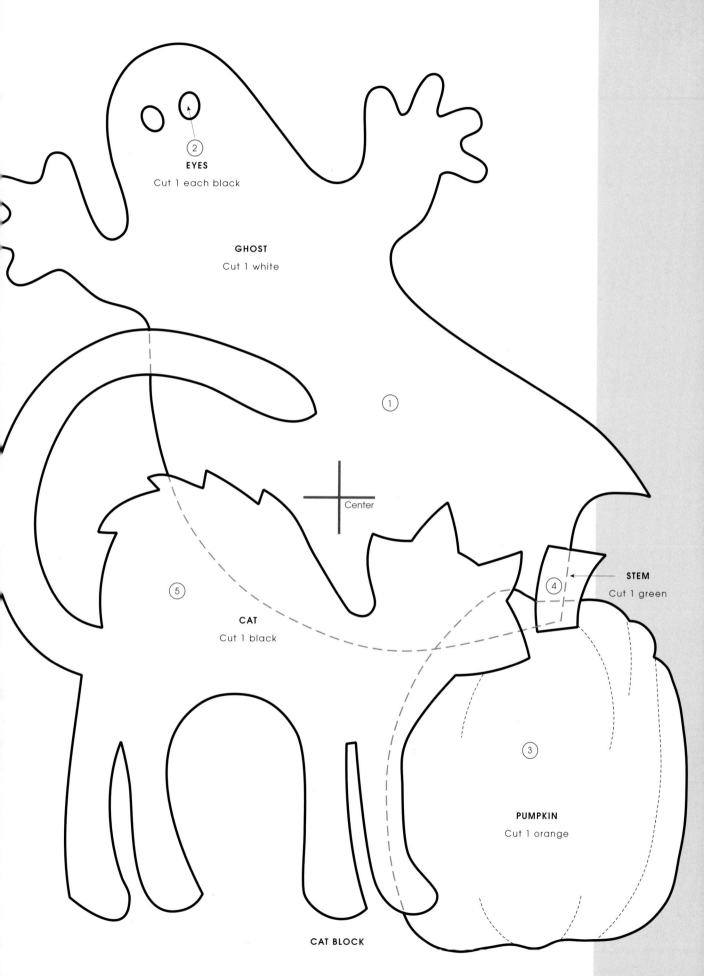

EYES
Cut 1 each black

GHOST
Cut 1 white

CAT
Cut 1 black

STEM
Cut 1 green

PUMPKIN
Cut 1 orange

Center

CAT BLOCK

127

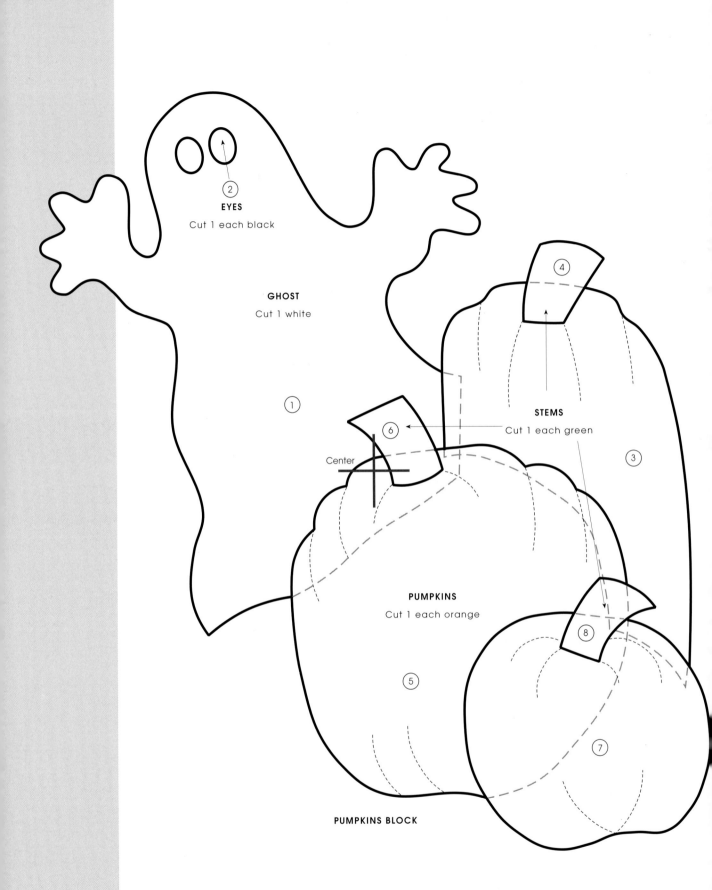

EYES
Cut 1 each black

②

GHOST
Cut 1 white

①

STEMS
Cut 1 each green

④

③

⑥

Center

PUMPKINS
Cut 1 each orange

⑧

⑤

⑦

PUMPKINS BLOCK

HANDLE
Cut 1 brown

HAND
Cut 1 peach

HAT
Cut 1 black

FACE
Cut 1
peach

HAIR
Cut 1
each
orange

SLEEVE
Cut 1 black

Center

DRESS
Cut 1 black

SHOES
Cut 1 each
black

BROOM
Cut 1 yellow

WITCH BLOCK

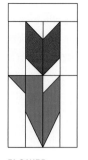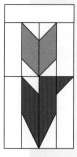

FLOWER
8" x 16" Block

REVERSED FLOWER
8" x 16" Block

Song of Spring

DESIGN > BEA YURKERWICH

Pieced tulips in a variety of colors seem to sing in this lap-size quilt.

PROJECT SPECIFICATIONS

Skill Level: Intermediate
Quilt Size: 45" x 55"
Block Size: 8" x 16"
Number of Blocks: 12

MATERIALS

- Scraps of 12 bright prints or tonals
- Scraps of 12 green prints or tonals
- 1⅓ yards cream tonal
- 1½ yards aqua floral
- 1⅔ yards aqua tonal
- Backing 51" x 61"
- Batting 51" x 61"
- Neutral color all-purpose thread
- Quilting thread
- Basic sewing tools and supplies

INSTRUCTIONS

Cutting

Step 1. Prepare templates for F and G using pattern pieces given; cut as directed on each piece for one block. Repeat for 12 blocks.

Step 2. Cut two 2½" x 6½" A rectangles from each bright scrap.

Step 3. Cut one 2½" x 2½" B square from each green scrap; draw a diagonal line from corner to corner on the wrong side of each square.

Step 4. Cut four 2½" by fabric width strips cream tonal; subcut into (24) 6½" C segments.

Step 5. Cut eight 2½" by fabric width strips cream tonal; subcut into (36) 8½" D segments.

Step 6. Cut four 2½" by fabric width strips cream tonal; subcut into (60) 2½" E squares. Draw a diagonal line on the wrong side of each square.

Step 7. Cut three 2½" x 48½" H strips along length of aqua floral.

Step 8. Cut five 2¼"-wide strips along length of aqua floral for binding.

Step 9. Cut two 4" x 48½" I strips and two 4" x 45½" J strips along length of aqua tonal.

Piecing the Blocks

Step 1. To piece one block, sew F and FR to same-green G and GR pieces; press seams toward G and GR.

Step 2. Place a same-green B right sides together on one corner of D, stitch on the marked line, trim seam allowance to ¼" and press B to the right side to complete one B-D unit as shown in **Figure 1**.

FIGURE 1 Complete 1 B-D unit.

Step 3. Repeat Step 2 with five E squares, two same-bright A pieces and the FR-GR unit to complete one A-E unit, one reversed A-E unit and one E-FR-GR unit as shown in **Figure 2**.

FIGURE 2 Complete A-E,
reversed A-E and E-FR-GR units.

Step 4. Sew the A-E unit to the reversed A-E unit as shown in **Figure 3**; press seam toward the reversed unit. Add C to opposite sides and D to the top to complete the flower

unit, again referring to **Figure 3**; press seams toward A-E units.

FIGURE 3 Complete a flower unit.

Step 5. Sew F-G to E-FR-GR as shown in Figure 4; press seam toward F-G. Add B-D and D to opposite sides of the pieced unit to complete the leaf unit, again referring to **Figure 4**; press seams toward B-D and D.

FIGURE 4 Complete a leaf unit.

Step 6. Join the flower unit with the leaf unit to complete one Flower block as shown in **Figure 5**; press seam toward the leaf unit. Repeat to make eight Flower blocks using same-bright A pieces and same-green B, G and GR pieces in each block.

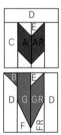

FIGURE 5 Join the flower unit with the leaf unit to complete 1 Flower block.

Step 7. Repeat Steps 1–6 to make four Reversed Flower blocks referring to **Figure 6** for positioning of B, G and GR pieces.

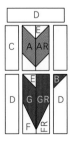

FIGURE 6 Complete a Reversed Flower block as shown.

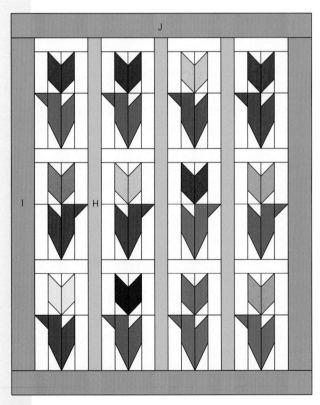

SONG OF SPRING Placement Diagram 45" x 55"

Completing the Top

Step 1. Join two Flower blocks with one Reversed Flower block to make a vertical row as shown in **Figure 7**; press seams toward D. Repeat for four rows.

FIGURE 7 Join 2 Flower blocks with 1 Reversed Flower block to make a vertical row.

Step 2. Join the rows with the H strips; press seams toward H.

Step 3. Sew I to opposite sides and J to the top and bottom of the pieced center to complete the top; press seams toward I and J.

Finishing the Quilt

Step 1. Sandwich the batting between the completed top and prepared backing; pin or baste layers together to hold.

Step 2. Hand- or machine-quilt as desired. When quilting is complete, trim batting and backing even with top; remove pins or basting.

Step 3. Join the previously cut binding strips on short ends to make one long strip. Fold the strip in half along length with wrong sides together; press.

Step 4. Sew binding to quilt edges, mitering corners and overlapping ends. Fold binding to the backside and stitch in place. ◆

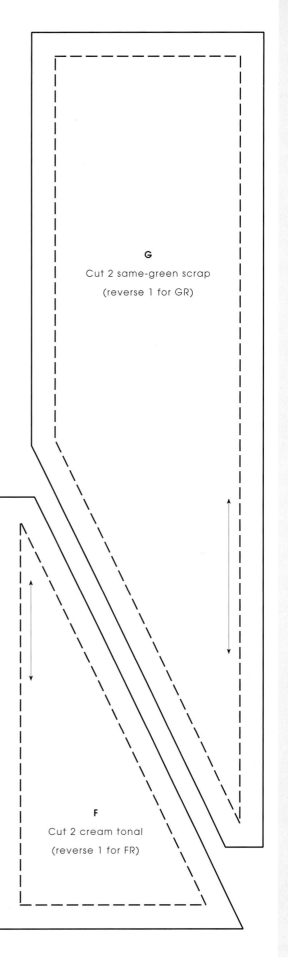

G
Cut 2 same-green scrap
(reverse 1 for GR)

F
Cut 2 cream tonal
(reverse 1 for FR)

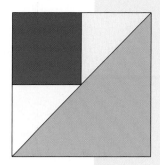

SQUARES & TRIANGLES
8" x 8" Block

Squares & Triangles

DESIGN > RUTH SWASEY

Dig out those blue, green and cream scraps to make this simple-to-stitch bed-size quilt.

PROJECT SPECIFICATIONS
Skill Level: Beginner
Quilt Size: 94" x 94"
Block Size: 8" x 8"
Number of Blocks: 121

MATERIALS
- 61 different 8⅞" x 8⅞" squares medium and dark green and blue prints or tonals for A
- 121 different 4½" x 4½" squares medium and dark green and blue prints or tonals for B
- 121 different 4⅞" x 4⅞" light prints or tonals for C
- 10 different 2¼" by fabric width strips blue prints or tonals for binding
- 1 yard white print for border
- Backing 100" x 100"
- Batting 100" x 100"
- Neutral color all-purpose thread
- Quilting thread
- Basic tools and supplies

INSTRUCTIONS
Piecing Blocks
Step 1. Cut each A and C square in half on one diagonal to make A and C triangles. Set aside one A triangle for another use.

Step 2. To piece one block, select one A and two C triangles and one B square.

Step 3. Sew C to two adjacent sides of B as shown in **Figure 1**; press seams toward B.

FIGURE 1 Sew C to 2 adjacent sides of B.

Step 4. Sew the B-C unit to A as shown in **Figure 2** to complete one block; press seam toward A. Repeat for 121 blocks.

FIGURE 2 Sew the B-C unit to A.

Step 5. Select 11 blocks; arrange and join the blocks to make a row as shown in **Figure 3**; repeat for 11 rows. Press seams in one direction.

FIGURE 3 Join 11 blocks to make a row.

Step 6. Join the rows to complete the pieced center; press seams in one direction.

Step 7. Cut nine 3½" by fabric width strips white print; join strips on short ends to make one long strip. Press seams to one side.

Step 8. Cut strip into two 88½" D and two 94½" E strips.

Step 9. Sew a D strip to opposite sides and an E strip to the top and bottom of the pieced center to complete the quilt top. Press seams toward D and E strips.

Finishing the Quilt

Step 1. Sandwich the batting between the completed top and prepared backing piece; pin or baste to hold.

Step 2. Hand- or machine-quilt as desired.

Step 3. Trim batting and backing even with the quilted top.

Step 4. Join the binding strips on short ends with a diagonal seam to make a long strip; press seams toward one side.

Step 5. Press the strip in half along length with wrong sides together to complete the binding strip. Bind edges of quilt to finish. ◆

SQUARES & TRIANGLES Placement Diagram 94" x 94"

STRIPPY SCRAP
10" x 10" Block

Tic-Tac-Toe

DESIGN > JULIE WEAVER

Add triangles to the corners of strippy squares and then add

sashing and the results look like a Tic-Tac-Toe game.

PROJECT SPECIFICATIONS

Skill Level: Beginner
Quilt Size: 64" x 78"
Block Size: 10" x 10"
Number of Blocks: 20

MATERIALS

- 20 (11" x 11") squares paper or muslin
  for foundations
- Scraps of a variety of medium-to-dark
  flannel for blocks
- 1⅜ yards rust mottled flannel
- 2¼ yards total assorted cream flannel scraps
- 2¼ yards rust tonal flannel
- Backing 70" x 84"
- Batting 70" x 84"
- Neutral color all-purpose thread
- Quilting thread
- Basic tools and supplies

INSTRUCTIONS
Cutting
Step 1. Cut medium-to-dark flannel scraps that vary from 1"–2" wide and up to 16½" long.

Step 2. Cut (356) 2½" x 2½" B squares and (30) 4½" x 4½" C squares from assorted cream flannel scraps.

Step 3. Cut (17) 4½" by fabric width strips rust tonal; subcut strips into (49) 10½" D rectangles.

Step 4. Cut (10) 2½" by fabric width strips rust mottled; subcut strips into (22) 4½" E rectangles and (18) 10½" F rectangles.

Step 5. Cut two 2⅞" x 2⅞" G squares each rust mottled and cream scraps; cut each square in half to make G triangles.

Step 6. Cut eight 2¼" by fabric width strips rust mottled for binding.

Piecing Blocks

Step 1. Place a long 1"–2" strip right side up on the diagonal on a foundation square as shown in **Figure 1**. Select a second strip and place right sides together on the first strip as shown in **Figure 2**; do not line up raw edges. Sew in place; trim strip 1 seam allowance away from behind strip 2 to reduce bulk. Press strip 2 to the right side. *Note: Sewing the strips in a slightly off manner adds to the interest of the block and gives the quilt a strippy look.*

FIGURE 1 Place strip 1 on the foundation as shown.

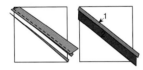

FIGURE 2 Place strip 2 on strip 1 and stitch; trim excess strip 1 and press 2 to the right side.

Step 2. Select another strip and sew to the opposite side of strip 1 as for strip 2. Trim and press.

Step 3. Continue adding strips until the entire foundation is covered as shown in **Figure 3**.

FIGURE 3 Cover the foundation with strips.

Step 4. Trim square to 10½" x 10½" for A; repeat for 20 A squares.

Step 5. If using paper foundations, remove paper at this time.

Step 6. Draw a line from corner to corner on the wrong side of each B square.

Step 7. Pin and stitch a B square to each corner of A, sewing on the marked line as shown in **Figure 4**; trim seam to ¼" and press B to the right side to complete one Strippy Scrap block. Repeat for 20 blocks.

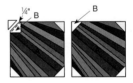

FIGURE 4 Pin B to each corner of A; sew on the marked line. Trim seam to ¼"; press B to the right side to complete 1 block.

Completing the Top

Step 1. Sew a B square to each corner of D as in Step 7 of Piecing Blocks to complete a B-D unit as shown in **Figure 5**; repeat for 49 units.

FIGURE 5 Complete a B-D unit as shown.

Step 2. Sew a B square to two corners of each E and F rectangle to make B-E and B-F units as shown in **Figure 6**.

FIGURE 6 Complete B-E and B-F units as shown.

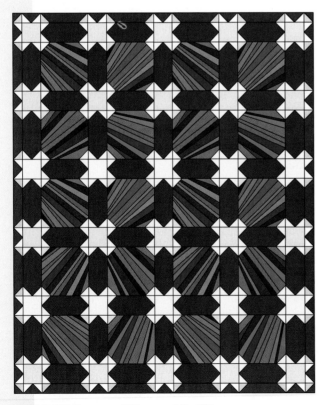

TIC-TAC-TOE Placement Diagram 64" x 78"

Step 3. Join four blocks with two B-F and five B-D units to make a block row as shown in **Figure 7**; repeat for five block rows. Press seams toward B-D units.

FIGURE 7 Join 4 blocks with 2 B-F and 5 B-D units to make a block row.

Step 4. Join two B-E units with four B-D units and five C squares to make a sashing row referring to **Figure 8**; repeat to make six sashing rows. Press seams toward C.

FIGURE 8 Join 2 B-E units with 4 B-D units and 5 C squares to make a sashing row.

Step 5. Sew a cream G to a rust mottled G to make a G unit as shown in **Figure 9**; repeat for four G units.

FIGURE 9 Complete G units.

Step 6. Join two G units with five B-E units and four B-F units to make a top row as shown in **Figure 10**; repeat for bottom row. Press seams away from B-E units.

FIGURE 10 Join 2 G units with 4 B-F and 5 B-E units to make a top row.

Step 7. Arrange top and bottom rows with block and sashing rows referring to the Placement Diagram for positioning of rows; join to complete the pieced top. Press seams toward sashing rows.

Finishing the Quilt
Step 1. Sandwich the batting between the completed top and prepared backing piece; pin or baste to hold.
Step 2. Hand- or machine-quilt as desired.
Step 3. Trim batting and backing even with the quilted top.

Step 4. Join the binding strips on short ends with a diagonal seam to make a long strip; press seams toward one side.
Step 5. Press the strip in half along length with wrong sides together to complete the binding strip. Bind edges of quilt to finish. ◆

Triangle

Plaids

DESIGN > CONNIE KAUFFMAN

A variety of woven and printed plaids are used to create movement in this bed-size quilt.

PROJECT SPECIFICATIONS

Skill Level: Intermediate
Quilt Size: 78" x 104"

MATERIALS

- 80 (7³⁄₈" x 7³⁄₈") light plaid squares for A
- 80 (7³⁄₈" x 7³⁄₈") dark plaid squares for B
- ⅔ yard dark plaid for binding
- 1 yard total red and rust scraps for borders
- 1 yard total dark green scraps for borders
- Backing 84" x 110"
- Batting 84" x 110"
- Neutral color all-purpose thread
- Quilting thread
- Basic tools and supplies

INSTRUCTIONS

Step 1. Cut each A and B square in half on one diagonal to make 160 A and 160 B triangles.

Step 2. Sew A to B to complete an A-B unit as shown in **Figure 1**; repeat for 148 A-B units. Press seams toward B.

FIGURE 1 Sew A-B and A-A units as shown.

Step 3. Sew A to A to complete an A-A unit, again referring to **Figure 1**; repeat for four A-A units. Press seams to one side.

Step 4. Cut four 4" x 23" C strips dark green scraps and four 3½" x 23" D strips red or rust scraps.

Step 5. Sew a C strip to a D strip with right sides together along length; press seams to one side. Repeat for four C-D strips.

Step 6. Align a B triangle on one end of a C-D strip as shown in **Figure 2**; stitch along the diagonal of B and press B to the right side. Trim away excess C-D from behind B as shown in

FIGURE 2 Align a B triangle on 1 end of a C-D strip.

Figure 3. Repeat for two B-C-D and two B-C-D reversed strips.

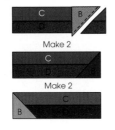

FIGURE 3 Trim away excess C-D from behind B.

Step 7. Join one B-C-D and one B-C-D reversed strip as shown in **Figure 4** to make a top border strip; press seams open. Repeat for a bottom border strip.

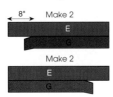

FIGURE 4 Join 1 B-C-D and 1 B-C-D reversed strip.

Step 8. Cut six 4" x 26½" E strips dark green scraps and two 3½" x 26½" F strips red or rust scraps. Cut four 3½" x 20" G strips red or rust scraps.

Step 9. Sew an E strip to a G strip with right sides together along length, leaving 8" from the end of E unstitched as shown in **Figure 5**. Repeat for four E-G strips.

FIGURE 5 Sew an E strip to a G strip with right sides together along length, leaving 8" from the end unstitched.

Step 10. Sew a B triangle to one end of each strip referring to Step 6 and **Figure 6** to make two B-E-G and two B-E-G reversed strips.

FIGURE 6 Make B-E-G and B-E-G reversed strips.

Step 11. Sew an E strip to an F strip with right sides together along length; press seam to one side. Repeat for two E-F strips.

Step 12. Sew a B triangle to each end of the E-F strips as shown in **Figure 7** to make two B-B-E-F strips.

FIGURE 7 Sew B to each end of E-F.

Step 13. Join one B-E-G strip and one B-E-G reversed strip with a B-B-E-F strip as shown **Figure 8** to make a side border strip; press seams open. Repeat for two strips.

FIGURE 8 Join 1 B-E-G strip and 1 B-E-G reversed strip with a B-B-E-F strip to make side border strip.

Step 14. Lay out the A-A and A-B units, A triangles and border strips as shown in **Figure 9**. *Note: The A-A units are in the inner corners and the A triangles form the outer corners.* Join center A-B and A-A units to make rows; join rows to complete the pieced center.

FIGURE 9 Lay out blocks and border strips as shown.

Step 15. Sew the B-C-D strips to the top and bottom of the pieced center; press seams toward B-C-D.

Step 16. Sew a side border strip to opposite sides of the pieced center; finish unstitched seam between E and G strips at ends and complete side seam as shown in **Figure 10**. Press seams toward side border strips.

FIGURE 10 Finish unstitched seam between E and G strips at ends and complete side seam.

Step 17. Join side A-B units to make rows; join rows and sew to opposite sides of the pieced center; press seams toward side border strips.
Step 18. Join top and bottom A triangles and A-B units to make rows; join rows and sew to the top and bottom of the pieced center; press seams toward B-C-D strips to complete the pieced top.

Finishing the Quilt
Step 1. Sandwich the batting between the completed top and prepared backing piece; pin or baste to hold.
Step 2. Hand- or machine-quilt as desired.
Step 3. Trim batting and backing even with the quilted top.
Step 4. Cut nine 2¼" by fabric width strips dark plaid for binding.
Step 5. Join the binding strips on short ends with a diagonal seam to make a long strip; press seams toward one side.

TRIANGLE PLAIDS Placement Diagram 78" x 104"

Step 6. Press the strip in half along length with wrong sides together to complete the binding strip. Bind edges of quilt to finish. ◆

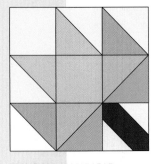

TAN/GOLD MAPLE LEAF

9" x 9" Block

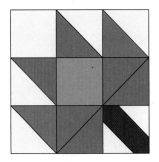

GREEN MAPLE LEAF

9" x 9" Block

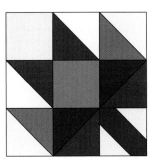

RUST/BROWN MAPLE LEAF

9" x 9" Block

Autumn Ridge
Lap Quilt

DESIGN > PEARL LOUISE KRUSH

Scraps in the colors of autumn leaves make a pretty seasonal lap quilt.

PROJECT SPECIFICATIONS

Skill Level: Beginner
Quilt Size: 53" x 71"
Block Size: 9" x 9"
Number of Blocks: 35

MATERIALS

- Scraps of 5 tan/gold fabrics to total
  1 yard
- Scraps of 5 green fabrics to total ¾ yard
- Scraps of 5 rust/brown fabrics to total
  ⅞ yard
- ½ yard brown print for stems
- ½ yard green mottled for borders
- ½ yard brown/rust print for binding
- ¾ yard autumn print for borders
- Scraps white/cream fabrics to total
  1¾ yards
- Backing 59" x 77"
- Batting 59" x 77"
- Neutral color all-purpose thread
- Quilting thread
- Basic sewing tools and supplies

INSTRUCTIONS

Cutting

Step 1. Cut 10 green, 12 brown/rust and 13 tan/gold 3½" x 3½" A squares and 35 white/cream 3½" x 3½" B squares.

Step 2. Cut 70 white/cream 3⅞" x 3⅞" C squares; cut each square in half on one diagonal to make C triangles.

Step 3. Cut 40 green, 48 rust and 52 gold 3⅞" x 3⅞" D squares; cut each square in half on one diagonal to make D triangles.

Step 4. Cut 35 brown print F squares 3½" x 3½".

Step 5. Cut 70 white/cream E squares 2½" x 2½"; draw a line from corner to corner on the wrong side of each square.

Step 6. Cut six strips 1½" by fabric width green mottled; join strips on short ends to make one long strip. Press seams open. Cut strip into two 63½" G strips and two 47½" H strips.

Step 7. Cut six strips 3½" by fabric width autumn print; join strips on short ends to make one long strip. Press seams to one side. Cut strip into two 65½" I strips and two 47½" J strips.

Step 8. Cut four 3½" x 3½" K squares green mottled.

Step 9. Cut seven 2¼" by fabric width strips brown/rust print for binding.

Piecing the Blocks

Step 1. Separate the cut pieces into piles by color families and shapes.

Step 2. To piece one green block, select four same-fabric pairs of D triangles.

Step 3. Sew C to D and D to D as shown in **Figure 1**; repeat for four C-D and two D-D units.

FIGURE 1 Sew C to D and D to D.

Step 4. Place an E square on F and stitch on the marked line as shown in **Figure 2**; trim seam to ¼" and press E to the right side. Repeat on the opposite corner of F with a second E to complete an E-F unit as shown in **Figure 3**.

FIGURE 2 Place an E square on F and stitch on the marked line; trim seam to ¼" and press E to the right side.

FIGURE 3 Repeat with a second E to complete an E-F unit.

Step 5. Arrange the C-D and D-D units with A and B squares and the E-F unit in rows as shown in **Figure 4**; join units to make rows. Press seams in adjacent rows in opposite directions.

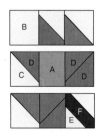

FIGURE 4 Arrange the C-D and D-D units with A and B squares and the E-F unit in rows; join to complete 1 block.

Step 6. Join the rows to complete one green Maple Leaf block, again referring to **Figure 4**; press seams in one direction.

Step 7. Repeat with tan/gold, rust/brown and remaining green pieces to complete 10 green, 12 rust/brown and 13 tan/gold blocks.

Completing the Top

Step 1. Arrange blocks in seven rows of five blocks each referring to the Placement Diagram for positioning of blocks. ***Note:*** *In the sample quilt, the blocks are arranged with same-color blocks creating diagonal rows across the quilt top.*

Step 2. Join blocks in rows; press seams in adjacent rows in opposite directions. Join the rows to complete the pieced center; press seams in one direction.

Step 3. Sew a G strip to opposite long sides and H strips to the top and bottom of the pieced center; press seams toward strips.

Step 4. Sew an I strip to opposite long sides of the pieced center; press seams toward I.

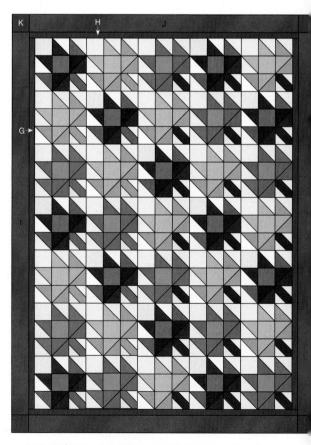

AUTUMN RIDGE LAP QUILT Placement Diagram 53" x 71"

Step 5. Sew a K square to each end of each J strip; press seams toward J. Sew a J-K strip to the top and bottom of the pieced center; press seams toward J-K strips.

Finishing the Quilt

Step 1. Sandwich the batting between the completed top and prepared backing; pin or baste layers together to hold.

Step 2. Hand- or machine-quilt as desired. When quilting is complete, trim batting and backing even with top; remove pins or basting.

Step 3. Join the previously cut binding strips on short ends to make one long strip. Fold the strip in half along length with wrong sides together; press.

Step 4. Sew binding to quilt edges, mitering corners and overlapping ends. Fold binding to the backside and stitch in place to finish. ◆

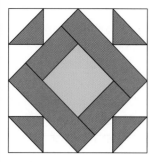

MOSAIC MEMORIES

8" x 8" Block

Mosaic
Memories

DESIGN > JILL REBER

The quilting lines create the appearance of seams where there are none in this easy lap-size quilt.

PROJECT SPECIFICATIONS

Skill Level: Beginner
Quilt Size: 44" x 60"
Block Size: 8" x 8"
Number of Blocks: 24

MATERIALS

- 24 different novelty print A squares 3⅜" x 3⅜"
- 12 different 6" by fabric width strips bright fabrics for B and C pieces
- ½ yard binding fabric
- ¾ yard border print
- 1⅜ yards white solid
- Backing 50" x 66"
- Batting 50" x 66"
- Neutral color all-purpose thread
- Quilting thread
- Basic sewing tools and supplies

INSTRUCTIONS

Cutting

Step 1. Cut (11) 2⅞" by fabric width strips white solid; subcut into (144) 2⅞" D squares. Cut each square in half on one diagonal to make 288 D triangles.

Step 2. Referring to **Figure 1**, cut the following from each of the 12 different 6" by fabric width strip bright fabrics: four 1⅞" x 3⅜" B rectangles, four 1⅞" x 6⅛" C rectangles and two 2⅞" x 2⅞" E squares. Cut each E square in half on one diagonal to make four E triangles.

FIGURE 1 Cut pieces B, C and E from a bright fabric strip as shown.

Step 3. Cut five 2½" by fabric width strips white solid for F and G strips.

Step 4. Cut five 4½" by fabric width strips border print for H and I strips.

Step 5. Cut six 2¼" by fabric width strips binding fabric.

Piecing the Blocks

Step 1. To piece one block, select one set of bright color pieces and, referring to **Figure 2**, sew B to opposite sides of A; press seams toward B. Add C to remaining sides of A; press seams toward C.

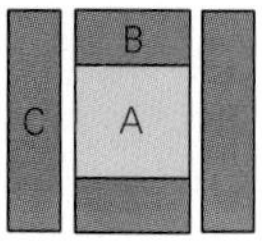

FIGURE 2 Sew B to opposite sides of A; add C.

Step 2. Join three D triangles with an E square to make a D-E unit as shown in **Figure 3**; press seams toward D pieces. Repeat for four D-E units.

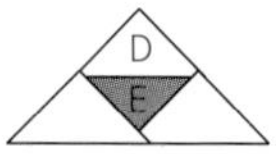

FIGURE 3 Join 3 D triangles with an E triangle to make a D-E unit.

Step 3. Join the D-E units with the A-B-C unit to complete one block; press seams toward the A-B-C unit. Repeat to make two blocks of each of the 12 fabrics to total 24 blocks.

Completing the Top
Step 1. Select three sets of same-fabric blocks; arrange in a vertical row as shown in **Figure 4**; repeat for four rows. Join the blocks to make rows; press seams of two rows in one direction and two rows in the opposite direction.

MOSAIC MEMORIES Placement Diagram 44" x 60"

FIGURE 4 Join blocks
in a vertical row.

Step 2. Join the rows to complete the pieced center; press seams in one direction.
Step 3. Join the F and G strips on short ends to make one long strip; subcut into two 32½" F strips and two 52½" G strips.
Step 4. Sew F to the top and bottom and G to opposite sides of the pieced center; press seams toward strips.
Step 5. Join the H and I strips on short ends to make one long strip; subcut strip into two 36½" H strips and two 60½" I strips.
Step 6. Sew H to the top and bottom and I to opposite sides of the pieced center; press seams toward strips to complete the pieced top.

Finishing the Quilt
Step 1. Sandwich the batting between the completed top and prepared backing; pin or baste layers together to hold.
Step 2. Hand- or machine-quilt as desired.

When quilting is complete, trim batting and backing even with top; remove pins or basting. *Note: The quilt shown was machine-quilted using variegated quilting thread in the blocks as shown in* **Figure 5** *to create an illusion of seams where there are none. The remainder of the background was machine-quilted with white thread in a meandering design.*

FIGURE 5 Blocks were
machine-quilted as shown.

Step 3. Join the previously cut binding strips on short ends to make one long strip. Fold the strip in half along length with wrong sides together; press.
Step 4. Sew binding to quilt edges, mitering corners and overlapping ends. Fold binding to the backside and stitch in place. ◆

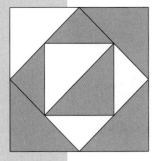

CIVIL WAR NOTES TO HOME

6" x 6" Block

Civil War
Notes to Home

DESIGN > RUTH SWASEY

Scraps of a variety of Civil War–era reproduction prints were used to create the blocks in this noteworthy quilt.

PROJECT SPECIFICATIONS

Skill Level: Beginner

Quilt Size: 33" x 39"

Block Size: 6" x 6"

Number of Blocks: 30

MATERIALS

- 1 yard total light prints
- 2 yards total dark prints
- Backing 39" x 45"
- Batting 39" x 45"
- Neutral color all-purpose thread
- Quilting thread
- Basic sewing tools and supplies

INSTRUCTIONS

Cutting

Step 1. Cut 30 light print and 60 dark print 3⅞" x 3⅞" squares. Cut each square in half on one diagonal to make 60 light A triangles and 120 dark A triangles.

Step 2. Cut 30 B squares each light and dark prints 3" x 3". Cut each square in half on one diagonal to make 60 B triangles each light and dark prints.

Step 3. Cut two 2" x 36½" C strips and two 2" x 33½" D strips dark print.

Step 4. Cut four 2¼" by fabric width strips dark print for binding.

Piecing the Blocks

Step 1. To piece one block, sew a light A to a dark A along the diagonal edges; press seams toward darker fabric. ***Note:*** *In the sample, the same dark and light prints were used to cut the A and B pieces in each individual block. Some fabrics were repeated in more than one block.*

Step 2. Sew two each light and dark B triangles to the sides of the A unit as shown in **Figure 1**; press seams toward darker fabrics.

FIGURE 1 Sew 2 each light and dark B triangles to the sides of the A unit.

CIVIL WAR NOTES TO HOME Placement Diagram 33" x 39"

Step 3. Sew one light and three dark A triangles to sides of the A-B unit to complete one block as shown in **Figure 2**; press seams toward darker fabrics.

FIGURE 2 Sew 1 light and 3 dark A triangles to sides of the A-B unit to complete 1 block.

Completing the Top

Step 1. Join five blocks to make a row referring to **Figure 3** for positioning of light A pieces; press seams in one direction. Repeat for six rows.

FIGURE 3 Join 5 blocks to make a row.

Step 2. Join the rows to complete the pieced center; press seams in one direction.

Step 3. Sew a C strip to opposite sides and a D strip to the top and bottom of the pieced center; press seams toward C and D.

Finishing the Quilt

Step 1. Sandwich the batting between the completed top and prepared backing; pin or baste layers together to hold.

Step 2. Hand- or machine-quilt as desired. When quilting is complete, trim batting and backing even with top; remove pins or basting.

Step 3. Join the previously cut binding strips on short ends to make one long strip. Fold the strip in half along length with wrong sides together; press.

Step 4. Sew binding to quilt edges, mitering corners and overlapping ends. Fold binding to the backside and stitch in place. ◆

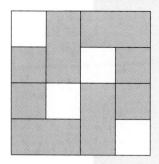

CRAZY EIGHTS
12" x 12" Block

Crazy Eights

DESIGN > RUTH M. SWASEY

Lots of scraps from the brown/gold/orange families were used to create this autumn-looking bed quilt.

PROJECT SPECIFICATIONS
Skill Level: Beginner
Quilt Size: 96" x 108"
Block Size: 12" x 12"
Number of Blocks: 56

MATERIALS
- 57 different 3½" by fabric width print strips for A and B pieces
- ⅔ yard brown print
- 5½ yards cream mottled
- Backing 102" x 114"
- Batting 102" x 114"
- Neutral color all-purpose thread
- Quilting thread
- Basic tools and supplies

INSTRUCTIONS
Cutting
Step 1. Cut four 6½" A rectangles from each fabric-width strip.
Step 2. Cut a 15" length from the remainder of each strip for B.

Step 3. Cut two 6½" x 84½" D strips and two 6½" x 96½" E strips along the length of the cream mottled.

Step 4. Cut five 3½" by fabric length C strips from remaining cream mottled.

Step 5. Cut (10) 2¼" by fabric width strips brown print for binding.

Piecing Blocks

Step 1. Sew a B strip to a C strip with right sides together along length; add B strips as one ends to cover complete length of C as shown in **Figure 1**. Press seams toward B. Repeat with all B and C strips.

FIGURE 1 Sew a B strip to a C strip; continue adding B strips to cover C.

Step 2. Subcut strip sets into four 3½" B-C units from each fabric. You will need four matching-fabric B-C units for each block and four for corner units or a total of 228 units.

Step 3. To piece one block, select four matching A pieces and four matching B-C units. Sew a B-C unit to A as shown in **Figure 2**; press seams toward A. Repeat for four A-B-C units.

FIGURE 2 Sew a B-C unit to A.

Step 4. Join four matching A-B-C units as shown in **Figure 3** to complete one block; press. Repeat for 56 blocks. You should have four matching A-B-C units left for border corner units.

FIGURE 3 Join 4 matching A-B-C units to complete 1 block.

Completing the Top

Step 1. Arrange blocks in eight rows of seven blocks each referring to the Placement Diagram for orientation of blocks in rows; join blocks in rows. Press seams in adjoining rows in opposite directions. Join rows to complete the pieced center.

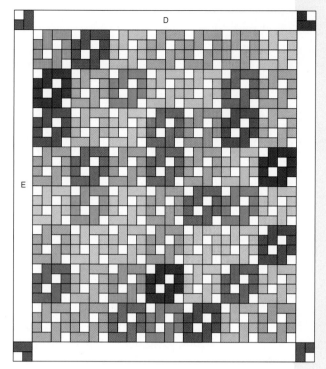

CRAZY EIGHTS Placement Diagram 96" x 108"

Step 2. Sew D strips to the top and bottom of the pieced center; press seams toward D.

Step 3. Sew an A-B-C corner unit to each end of each E strip referring to **Figure 4**; press seams toward E.

FIGURE 4 Sew an A-B-C corner unit to each end of each E strip.

Step 4. Sew the E strip with corner units to opposite long sides of the pieced center to complete the pieced top; press seams toward E.

Finishing the Quilt

Step 1. Sandwich the batting between the completed top and prepared backing piece; pin or baste to hold.

Step 2. Hand- or machine-quilt as desired.

Step 3. Trim batting and backing even with the quilted top.

Step 4. Join the binding strips on short ends with a diagonal seam to make a long strip; press seams toward one side.

Step 5. Press the strip in half along length with wrong sides together to complete the binding strip. Bind edges of quilt to finish. ◆

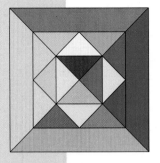

FOUR SEASONS
12" x 12" Block

Four
Seasons

DESIGN > CARLA SCHWAB

Choose scraps with lots of contrast to create the blocks in this scrappy quilt.

PROJECT SPECIFICATIONS
Skill Level: Beginner
Quilt Size: 36" x 48"
Block Size: 12" x 12"
Number of Blocks: 12

MATERIALS
- Scraps of 3 or more blue, gold and tan prints
- Scraps of 4 or more light and dark green prints
- Scraps of 4 different yellow solids from medium to dark
- ½ yard dark print for binding
- Backing 42" x 54"
- Batting 42" x 54"
- Neutral color all-purpose thread
- Quilting thread
- Basic sewing tools and supplies

INSTRUCTIONS
Step 1. Prepare templates for A and B using patterns given. Cut as directed on each piece for one block; repeat for 12 blocks.

Step 2. Join three A triangles from one color group with one yellow A referring to the Placement Diagram and photo of quilt for color suggestions and to **Figure 1** for piecing. Repeat for four A units, one from each color group; press.

FIGURE 1 Join 4 A triangles to complete an A unit.

Step 3. Sew B to each A unit as shown in **Figure 2**; press seams toward B. *Note: Sew light green B pieces to the darker yellow A units and dark green B pieces to the lighter yellow A units.*

FIGURE 2 Sew B to an A unit.

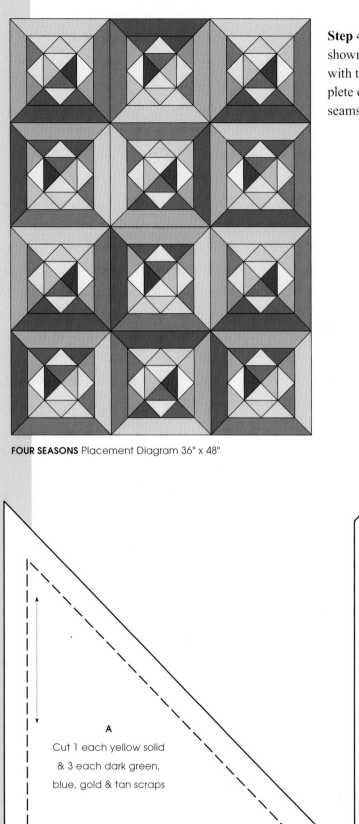

FOUR SEASONS Placement Diagram 36" x 48"

Step 4. Join two light green A-B units as shown in **Figure 3**; press seams open. Repeat with two dark green A-B units; join to complete one block as shown in **Figure 4**; press seams open.

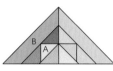

FIGURE 3 Join 2 A-B units.

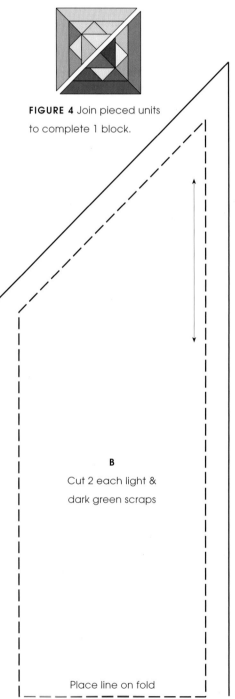

FIGURE 4 Join pieced units to complete 1 block.

A
Cut 1 each yellow solid
& 3 each dark green,
blue, gold & tan scraps

B
Cut 2 each light &
dark green scraps

Place line on fold

Step 5. Repeat Steps 1–4 to complete 12 blocks.

Step 6. Arrange blocks in four rows of three blocks each; press seams in one direction.

Step 7. Join the rows to complete the pieced top.

Finishing the Quilt

Step 1. Sandwich the batting between the completed top and prepared backing; pin or baste layers together to hold.

Step 2. Hand- or machine-quilt as desired.

When quilting is complete, trim batting and backing even with top; remove pins or basting.

Step 3. Cut five 2¼" by fabric width strips dark print for binding. Join strips on short ends to make one long strip. Fold the strip in half along length with wrong sides together; press.

Step 4. Sew binding to quilt edges, mitering corners and overlapping ends. Fold binding to the backside and stitch in place. ◆

General Instructions

Quiltmaking Basics

Materials & Supplies

Fabrics

Fabric Choices. Quilts and quilted projects combine fabrics of many types. Use same-fiber-content fabrics when making quilted items, if possible.

Buying Fabrics. One hundred percent cotton fabrics are recommended for making quilts. Choose colors similar to those used in the quilts shown or colors of your own preference. Most quilt designs depend more on contrast of values than on the colors used to create the design.

Preparing the Fabric for Use. Fabrics may be prewashed depending on your preference. Whether you prewash or not, be sure your fabrics are colorfast and won't run onto each other when washed after use.

Fabric Grain. Fabrics are woven with threads going in a crosswise and lengthwise direction. The threads cross at right angles—the more threads per inch, the stronger the fabric.

The crosswise threads will stretch a little. The lengthwise threads will not stretch at all. Cutting the fabric at a 45-degree angle to the crosswise and lengthwise threads produces a bias edge which stretches a great deal when pulled **(Figure 1)**.

If templates are given with patterns in this book, pay careful attention to the grain lines marked with arrows. These arrows indicate that the piece should be placed on the lengthwise grain with the arrow running on one thread. Although it is not necessary to examine the fabric and find a thread to match to, it is important to try to place the arrow with the lengthwise grain of the fabric **(Figure 2)**.

Thread

For most piecing, good-quality cotton or cotton-covered polyester is the thread of choice. Inexpensive polyester threads are not recommended because they can cut the fibers of cotton fabrics.

Choose a color thread that will match or blend with the fabrics in your quilt. For projects pieced with dark and light color fabrics choose a neutral thread color, such as a medium gray, as a compromise between colors. Test by pulling a sample seam.

Batting

Batting is the material used to give a quilt loft or thickness. It also adds warmth.

Batting size is listed in inches for each pattern to reflect the size needed to complete the quilt according to the instructions. Purchase the size large enough to cut the size you need for the quilt of your choice.

Some qualities to look for in batting are drapability, resistance to fiber migration, loft and softness.

Tools & Equipment

There are few truly essential tools and little equipment required for quiltmaking. Basics include needles (hand-sewing and quilting betweens), pins (long, thin, sharp pins are best), sharp scissors or shears, a thimble, template materials (plastic or cardboard), marking tools (chalk marker, water-erasable pen and a No. 2 pencil are a few) and a quilting frame or hoop. For piecing and/or quilting by machine, add a sewing machine to the list.

Other sewing basics such as a seam ripper, pincushion, measuring tape and an iron are also necessary. For choosing colors or quilting designs for your quilt, or for designing your own quilt, it is helpful to have on hand graph paper, tracing paper, colored pencils or markers, and a ruler.

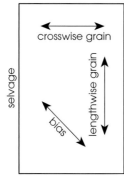

FIGURE 1 Drawing shows lengthwise, crosswise and bias threads.

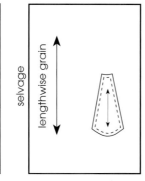

FIGURE 2 Place the template with marked arrow on the lengthwise grain of the fabric.

For making strip-pieced quilts, a rotary cutter, mat and specialty rulers are often used. We recommend an ergonomic rotary cutter, a large self-healing mat and several rulers. If you can choose only one size, a 6" x 24" marked in ⅛" or ¼" increments is recommended.

Construction Methods

Traditional Templates. While some quilt instructions in this book use rotary-cut strips and quick sewing methods, many patterns require a template. Templates are like the pattern pieces used to sew a garment. They are used to cut the fabric pieces that make up the quilt top. There are two types—templates that include a ¼" seam allowance and templates that don't.

Choose the template material and the pattern. Transfer the pattern shapes to the template material with a sharp No. 2 lead pencil. Write the pattern name, piece letter or number, grain line, and number to cut for one block or whole quilt on each piece as shown in **Figure 3**.

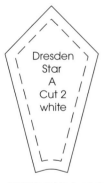

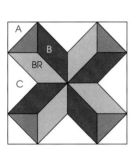

FIGURE 3 Mark each template with the pattern name and piece indentification.

FIGURE 4 This pattern uses reversed pieces.

Some patterns require a reversed piece as shown in **Figure 4**. These patterns are labeled with an R after the piece letter; for example, B and BR. To reverse a template, first cut it with the labeled side up and then with the labeled side down. Compare these to the right and left fronts of a blouse. When making a garment, you accomplish reversed pieces when cutting the pattern on two layers of fabric placed with right sides together. This can be done when cutting templates as well.

If cutting one layer of fabric at a time, first trace the template onto the backside of the fabric with the marked side down; turn the template over with the marked side up to make reverse pieces.

Hand-Piecing Basics. When hand-piecing it is easier to begin with templates that do not include the ¼" seam allowance. Place the template on the wrong side of the fabric, lining up the marked grain line with lengthwise or crosswise fabric grain. If the piece does not have to be reversed, place with labeled side up. Trace around shape; move, leaving ½" between the shapes, and mark again.

When you have marked the appropriate number of pieces, cut out pieces, leaving ¼" beyond marked line all around each piece.

To join two units, place the patches with right sides together. Stick a pin in at the beginning of the seam through both fabric patches, matching the beginning points (**Figure 5**); for hand-piecing, the seam begins on the traced line, not at the edge of the fabric (see **Figure 6**).

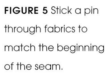

FIGURE 5 Stick a pin through fabrics to match the beginning of the seam.

FIGURE 6 Begin hand-piecing at seam, not at the edge of the fabric. Continue stitching along seam line.

Thread a sharp needle; knot one strand of the thread at the end. Remove the pin and insert the needle in the hole; make a short stitch and then a backstitch right over the first stitch. Continue making short stitches with several stitches on the needle at one time. As you stitch, check the back piece often to assure accurate stitching on the seam line. Take a stitch at the end of the seam; backstitch and knot at the same time as shown in **Figure 7**. Seams on hand-pieced fabric patches may be finger-pressed toward the darker fabric.

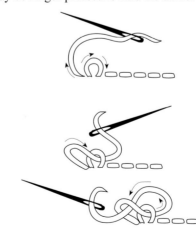

FIGURE 7 Make a loop in backstitch to make a knot.

To sew units together, pin fabric patches together, matching seams. Sew as above except where seams meet; at these intersections, backstitch, go through seam to next piece and backstitch again to secure seam joint.

Not all pieced blocks can be stitched with straight seams or in rows. Some patterns, such as star design, require set-in pieces. To begin a set-in seam, pin one side of the square to the proper side of the star point with right sides together, matching corners. Start stitching at the seam line on the outside point; stitch on the marked seam line to the end of the seam line at the center referring to **Figure 8**.

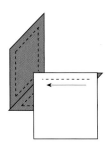

FIGURE 8 To set a square into a diamond point, match seams and stitch from outside edge to center.

Bring around the adjacent side and pin to the next star point, matching seams. Continue the stitching line from the adjacent seam through corners and to the outside edge of the square as shown in **Figure 9**.

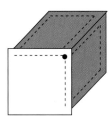

FIGURE 9 Continue stitching the adjacent side of the square to the next diamond shape in 1 seam from center to outside as shown.

Machine-Piecing. If making templates, include the ¼" seam allowance on the template for machine-piecing. Place template on the wrong side of the fabric as for hand-piecing except butt pieces against one another when tracing.

Set machine on 2.5 or 12–15 stitches per inch. Join pieces as for hand-piecing for set-in seams; but for other straight seams, begin and end sewing at the end of the fabric patch sewn as shown in **Figure 10**. No backstitching is necessary when machine-stitching.

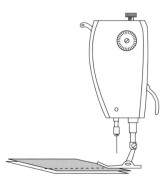

FIGURE 10 Begin machine-piecing at the end of the piece, not at the end of the seam.

Join units as for hand-piecing referring to the piecing diagrams where needed. Chain piecing (**Figure 11**—sewing several like units before sewing other units) saves time by eliminating beginning and ending stitches.

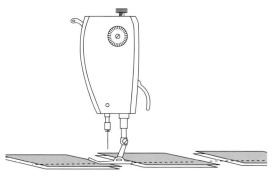

FIGURE 11 Units may be chain-pieced to save time.

When joining machine-pieced units, match seams against each other with seam allowances pressed in opposite directions to reduce bulk and make perfect matching of seams possible (**Figure 12**).

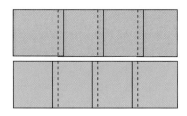

FIGURE 12 Sew machine-pieced units with seams pressed in opposite directions.

Quick-Cutting. Templates can be completely eliminated when using a rotary cutter with a plastic ruler and mat to cut fabric strips.

When rotary-cutting strips, straighten raw edges of fabric by folding fabric in fourths across the width as shown in **Figure 13**. Press down flat; place ruler on fabric square with edge of fabric and make one cut from the folded edge to the outside edge. If strips are not straightened, a wavy strip will result as shown in **Figure 14**.

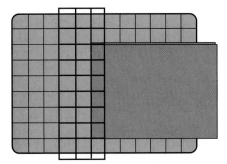

FIGURE 13 Fold fabric and straighten as shown.

FIGURE 14 Wavy strips result if fabric is not straightened before cutting.

Always cut away from your body, holding the ruler firmly with the non-cutting hand. Keep fingers away from the edge of the ruler as it is easy for the rotary cutter to slip and jump over the edge of the ruler if cutting is not properly done.

If a square is required for the pattern, it can be subcut from a strip as shown in **Figure 15**.

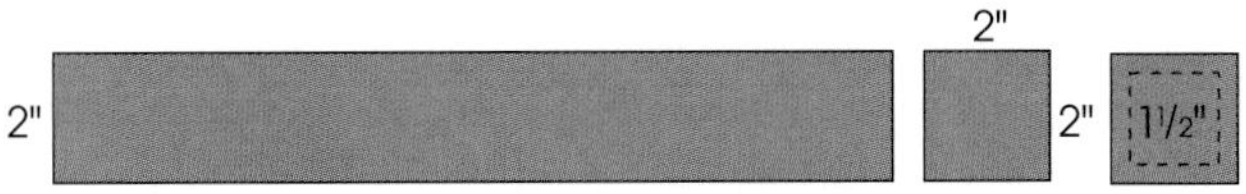

FIGURE 15 If cutting squares, cut proper-width strip into same-width segments. Here, a 2" strip is cut into 2" segments to create 2" squares. These squares finish at 1½" when sewn.

If you need right triangles with the straight grain on the short sides, you can use the same method, but you need to figure out how wide to cut the strip. Measure the finished size of one short side of the triangle. Add ⅞" to this size for seam allowance. Cut fabric strips this width; cut the strips into the same increment to create squares. Cut the squares on the diagonal to produce triangles. For example, if you need a triangle with a 2" finished height, cut the strips 2⅞" by the width of the fabric. Cut the strips into 2⅞" squares. Cut each square

on the diagonal to produce the correct-size triangle with the grain on the short sides (**Figure 16**).

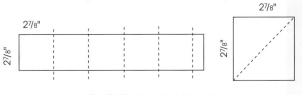

FIGURE 16 Cut 2" (finished size) triangles from 2⅞ squares as shown.

Triangles sewn together to make squares are called half-square triangles or triangle/squares. When joined, the triangle/square unit has the straight of grain on all outside edges of the block.

Another method of making triangle/squares is shown in **Figure 17**. Layer two squares with right sides together; draw a diagonal line through the center. Stitch ¼" on both sides of the line. Cut apart on the drawn line to reveal two stitched triangle/squares.

FIGURE 17 Mark a diagonal line on the square; stitch ¼" on each side of the line. Cut on line to reveal stitched triangle/squares.

If you need triangles with the straight of grain on the diagonal, such as for fill-in triangles on the outside edges of a diagonal-set quilt, the procedure is a bit different.

To make these triangles, a square is cut on both diagonals; thus, the straight of grain is on the longest or diagonal side (**Figure 18**). To figure out the size to cut the square, add 1¼" to the needed finished size of the longest side of the triangle. For example, if you need a triangle with a 12" finished diagonal, cut a 13¼" square.

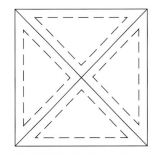

FIGURE 18 Add 1¼" to the finished size of the longest side of the triangle needed and cut on both diagonals to make a quarter-square triangle.

If templates are given, use their measurments to cut fabric strips to correspond with that measurement. The template may be used on the strip to cut pieces quickly. Strip cutting works best for squares, triangles, rectangles and diamonds. Odd-shaped templates are difficult to cut in multiple layers or using a rotary cutter.

Quick-Piecing Method. Lay pieces to be joined under the presser foot of the sewing machine right sides together. Sew an exact ¼" seam allowance to the end of the piece; place another unit right next to the first one and continue sewing, adding a piece after every stitched piece, until all of the pieces are used up (**Figure 19**).

FIGURE 19 Sew pieces together in a chain.

When sewing is finished, cut threads joining the pieces apart. Press seam toward the darker fabric.

Appliqué

Appliqué. Appliqué is the process of applying one piece of fabric on top of another for decorative or functional purposes.

Making Templates. Most appliqué designs given here are shown as full-size drawings for the completed designs. The drawings show dotted lines to indicate where one piece overlaps another. Other marks indicate placement of embroidery stitches for decorative purposes such as eyes, lips, flowers, etc.

For hand appliqué, trace each template onto the right side of the fabric with template right side up. Cut around shape, adding a ⅛"–¼" seam allowance.

Before the actual appliqué process begins, cut the background block. If you have a full-size drawing of the design, it might help you to transfer it to the background block to help with placement.

Transfer the design to a large piece of tracing paper. Place the paper on top of the design; use masking tape to hold in place. Trace design onto paper.

If you don't have a light box, tape the pattern on a window; center the background block on top and tape in place. Trace the design onto the background block with a water-erasable marker or light lead or chalk pencil. This drawing will mark exactly where the fabric pieces should be placed on the background block.

Hand Appliqué. Traditional hand appliqué uses a template made from the desired finished shape without seam allowance added.

After fabric is prepared, trace the desired shape onto the right side of the fabric with a water-erasable marker or light lead or chalk pencil. Leave at least ½" between design motifs when tracing to allow for the seam allowance when cutting out the shapes.

When the desired number of shapes needed has been drawn on the fabric pieces, cut out shapes leaving ⅛"–¼" all around drawn line for turning under.

Turn the shape's edges over on the drawn or stitched line. When turning in concave curves, clip to seams and baste the seam allowance over as shown in **Figure 20**.

Clip

FIGURE 20 Concave curves should be clipped before turning as shown.

During the actual appliqué process, you may be layering one shape on top of another. Where two fabrics overlap, the underneath piece does not have to be turned under or stitched down.

If possible, trim away the underneath fabric when the block is finished by carefully cutting away the background from underneath and then cutting away unnecessary layers to reduce bulk and avoid shadows from darker fabrics showing through on light fabrics.

For hand appliqué, position the fabric shapes on the background block and pin or baste them in place. Using a blind stitch or appliqué stitch, sew pieces in place with matching thread and small stitches. Start with background pieces first and work up to foreground pieces. Appliqué the pieces in place on the background in numerical order, if given, layering as necessary.

Machine Appliqué. There are several products available to help make the machine-appliqué process easier and faster.

Fusible transfer web is a commercial product similar to iron-on interfacings except it has two sticky sides. It is used to adhere appliqué shapes to the background with heat. Paper is adhered to one side of the web.

To use, reverse pattern and draw shapes onto the paper side of the web; cut, leaving a margin around each shape. Place on the wrong side of the chosen fabric; fuse in place referring to the manufacturer's instructions. Cut out shapes on the drawn line. Peel off the paper and fuse in place on the background fabric. Transfer any detail lines to the fabric shapes. This process adds a little bulk or stiffness to the appliquéd shape and makes hand-quilting through the layers difficult.

For successful machine appliqué a tear-off stabilizer is recommended. This product is placed under the background fabric while machine appliqué is being done. It is torn away when the work is finished. This kind of stabilizer keeps the background fabric from pulling during the machine-appliqué process.

During the actual machine-appliqué process, you will be layering one shape on top of another. Where two fabrics overlap, the underneath piece does not have to be turned under or stitched down.

Thread the top of the machine with thread to match the fabric patches or with threads that coordinate or contrast with fabrics. Rayon thread is a good choice when a sheen is desired on the finished appliqué stitches. Do not use rayon thread in the bobbin; use all-purpose thread.

When all machine work is complete, remove stabilizer from the back referring to the manufacturer's instructions.

Putting It All Together

Finishing the Top

Settings. Most quilts are made by sewing individual blocks together in rows that, when joined, create a design. There are several other methods used to join blocks. Sometimes the setting choice is determined by the block's design. For example, a House block should be placed upright on a quilt, not sideways or upside down.

Plain blocks can be alternated with pieced or appliquéd blocks in a straight set. Making a quilt using plain blocks saves time; half the number of pieced or appliquéd blocks are needed to make the same-size quilt as shown in **Figure 1**.

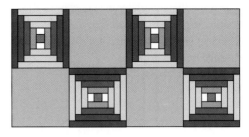

FIGURE 1 Alternate plain blocks with pieced blocks to save time.

Adding Borders. Borders are an integral part of the quilt and should complement the colors and designs used in the quilt center. Borders frame a quilt just like a mat and frame do a picture.

If fabric strips are added for borders, they may be mitered or butted at the corners as shown in **Figures 2** and **3**. To determine the size for butted border strips, measure across the center of the completed quilt top from one side raw edge to the other side raw edge. This measurement will include a ¼" seam allowance.

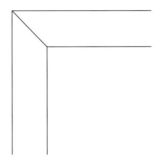

FIGURE 2 Mitered corners look like this.

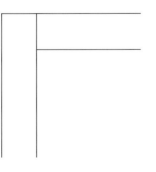

FIGURE 3 Butted corners look like this.

Cut two border strips that length by the chosen width of the border. Sew these strips to the top and bottom of the pieced center referring to **Figure 4**. Press the seam allowance toward the border strips.

Measure across the completed quilt top at the center, from top raw edge to bottom raw edge, including the two border strips already added. Cut two border strips that length by the chosen width of the border. Sew a strip to each of the two remaining sides as shown in **Figure 4**. Press the seams toward the border strips.

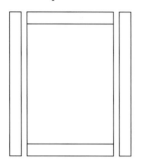

FIGURE 4 Sew border strips to opposite sides; sew remaining 2 strips to remaining sides to make butted corners.

To make mitered corners, measure the quilt as before. To this add twice the width of the border and ½" for seam allowances to determine the length of the strips. Repeat for opposite sides. Sew on each strip, stopping stitching ¼" from corner, leaving the remainder of the strip dangling.

Press corners at a 45-degree angle to form a crease. Stitch from the inside quilt corner to the outside on the creased line. Trim excess away after stitching and press mitered seams open (**Figures 5–7**).

FIGURE 5 For mitered corner, stitch strip, stopping ¼" from corner seam.

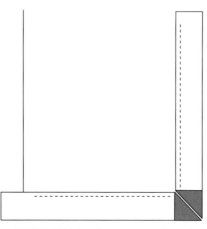

FIGURE 6 Fold and press corner to make a 45-degree angle.

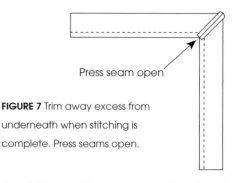

FIGURE 7 Trim away excess from underneath when stitching is complete. Press seams open.

Carefully press the entire piece, including the pieced center. Avoid pulling and stretching while pressing, which would distort shapes.

Getting Ready to Quilt

Choosing a Quilting Design. If you choose to hand- or machine-quilt your finished top, you will need to select a design for quilting.

There are several types of quilting designs, some of which may not have to be marked. The easiest of the unmarked designs is in-the-ditch quilting. Here the quilting stitches are placed in the valley created by the seams joining two pieces together or next to the edge of an appliqué design. There is no need to mark a top for in-the-ditch quilting. Machine quilters choose this option because the stitches are not as obvious on the finished quilt. (**Figure 8**).

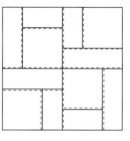

FIGURE 8 In-the-ditch quilting is done in the seam that joins 2 pieces.

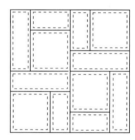

FIGURE 9 Outline-quilting ¼" away from seam is a popular choice for quilting.

Outline-quilting ¼" or more away from seams or appliqué shapes is another no-mark alternative (**Figure 9**) that prevents having to sew through the layers made by seams, thus making stitching easier.

If you are not comfortable eyeballing the ¼" (or other distance), masking tape is available in different widths and is helpful to place on straight-edge designs to mark the quilting line. If using masking tape, place the tape right up against the seam and quilt close to the other edge.

Meander or free-motion quilting by machine fills in open spaces and doesn't require marking. It is fun and easy to stitch as shown in **Figure 10**.

FIGURE 10 Machine meander quilting fills in large spaces.

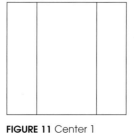

FIGURE 11 Center 1 backing piece with a piece on each side.

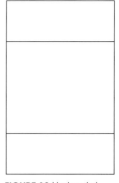

FIGURE 12 Horizontal seams may be used on backing pieces.

Marking the Top for Quilting. If you choose a fancy or allover design for quilting, you will need to transfer the design to your quilt top before layering with the backing and batting. You may use a sharp medium-lead or silver pencil on light background fabrics. Test the pencil marks to guarantee that they will wash out of your quilt top when quilting is complete; or be sure your quilting stitches cover the pencil marks. Mechanical pencils with very fine points may be used successfully to mark quilts.

Manufactured quilt-design templates are available in many designs and sizes and are cut out of a durable plastic template material that is easy to use.

To make a permanent quilt-design template, choose a template material on which to transfer the design. See-through plastic is the best as it will let you place the design while allowing you to see where it is in relation to your quilt design without moving it. Place the design on the quilt top where you want it and trace around it with your marking tool. Pick up the quilting template and place again; repeat marking.

No matter what marking method you use, remember—the marked lines should never show on the finished quilt. When the top is marked, it is ready for layering.

Preparing the Quilt Backing. The quilt backing is a very important feature of your quilt. The materials listed for each quilt in this book includes the size requirements for the backing, not the yardage needed. Exceptions to this are when the backing fabric is also used on the quilt top and yardage is given for that fabric.

A backing is generally cut at least 6" larger than the quilt top or 2" larger on all sides. For a 64" x 78" finished quilt, the backing would need to be at least 70" x 84".

To avoid having the seam across the center of the quilt backing, cut or tear one of the right-length pieces in half and sew half to each side of the second piece as shown in **Figure 11**.

Quilts that need a backing more than 88" wide may be pieced in horizontal pieces as shown in **Figure 12**.

Layering the Quilt Sandwich. Layering the quilt top with the batting and backing is time-consuming. Open the batting several days before you need it and place over a bed or flat on the floor to help flatten the creases caused from its being folded up in the bag for so long.

Iron the backing piece, folding in half both vertically and horizontally and pressing to mark centers.

If you will not be quilting on a frame, place the backing right side down on a clean floor or table. Start in the center and push any wrinkles or bunches flat. Use masking tape to tape the edges to the floor or large clips to hold the backing to the edges of the table. The backing should be taut.

Place the batting on top of the backing, matching centers using fold lines as guides; flatten out any wrinkles. Trim the batting to the same size as the backing.

Fold the quilt top in half lengthwise and place on top of the batting, wrong side against the batting, matching centers. Unfold quilt and, working from the center to the outside edges, smooth out any wrinkles or lumps.

To hold the quilt layers together for quilting, baste by hand or use safety pins. If basting by hand, thread a long thin needle with a long piece of unknotted white or off-white thread. Starting in the center and leaving a long tail, make 4"–6" stitches toward the outside edge of the quilt top, smoothing as you baste. Start at the center again and work toward the outside as shown in **Figure 13**.

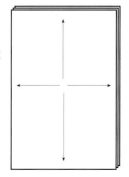

FIGURE 13 Baste from the center to the outside edges.

If quilting by machine, you may prefer to use safety pins for holding your fabric sandwich together. Start in the center of the quilt and pin to the outside, leaving pins open until all are placed. When you are satisfied that all layers are smooth, close the pins.

Quilting

Hand Quilting. Hand quilting is the process of placing stitches through the quilt top, batting and backing to hold them together. While it is a functional process, it also adds beauty and loft to the finished quilt.

To begin, thread a sharp between needle with an 18" piece of quilting thread. Tie a small knot in the end of the thread. Position the needle about ½" to 1" away from the starting point on quilt top. Sink the needle through the top into the batting layer but not through the backing. Pull the needle up at the starting point of the quilting design. Pull the needle and thread until the knot sinks through the top into the batting (**Figure 14**).

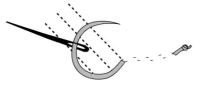

FIGURE 14 Start the needle through the top layer of fabric ½"-1" away from quilting line with knot on top of fabric.

Some stitchers like to take a backstitch here at the beginning while others prefer to begin the first stitch here. Take small, even running stitches along the marked quilting line (**Figure 15**). Keep one hand positioned underneath to feel the needle go all the way through to the backing.

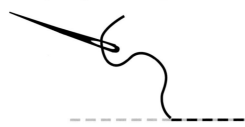

FIGURE 15 Make small, even running stitches on marked quilting line.

When you have nearly run out of thread, wind the thread around the needle several times to make a small knot and pull it close to the fabric. Insert the needle into the fabric on the quilting line and come out with the needle ½" to 1" away, pulling

the knot into the fabric layers the same as when you started. Pull and cut thread close to fabric. The end should disappear inside after cutting. Some quilters prefer to take a backstitch with a loop through it for a knot to end.

Machine Quilting. Successful machine quilting requires practice and a good relationship with your sewing machine.

Prepare the quilt for machine quilting in the same way as for hand quilting. Use safety pins to hold the layers together instead of basting with thread.

Presser-foot quilting is best used for straight-line quilting because the presser bar lever does not need to be continually lifted.

Set the machine on a longer stitch length (3.0 or 8–10 stitches to the inch). Too tight a stitch causes puckering and fabric tucks, either on the quilt top or backing. An even-feed or walking foot helps to eliminate the tucks and puckering by feeding the upper and lower layers through the machine evenly. Before you begin, loosen the amount of pressure on the presser foot.

Special machine-quilting needles work best to penetrate the three layers in your quilt.

Decide on a design. Quilting in the ditch is not quite as visible, but if you quilt with the feed dogs engaged, it means turning the quilt frequently. It is not easy to fit a rolled-up quilt through the small opening on the sewing machine head.

Meander quilting is the easiest way to machine-quilt—and it is fun. Meander quilting is done using an appliqué or darning foot with the feed dogs dropped. It is sort of like scribbling. Simply move the quilt top around under the foot and make stitches in a random pattern to fill the space. The same method may be used to outline a quilt design. The trick is the same as in hand quilting; you are striving for stitches of uniform size. Your hands are in complete control of the design.

If machine quilting is of interest to you, there are several very good books available at quilt shops that will help you become a successful machine quilter.

Finishing the Edges

After your quilt is tied or quilted, the edges need to be finished. Decide how you want the edges of your quilt finished before layering the backing and batting with the quilt top.

Without Binding—Self-Finish. There is one way to eliminate adding an edge finish. This is done before quilting. Place the batting on a flat surface. Place the pieced top right side up on the batting. Place the backing right sides together with the pieced top. Pin and/or baste the layers together to hold flat referring to Layering the Quilt Sandwich.

Begin stitching in the center of one side using a ¼" seam allowance, reversing at the beginning and end of the seam. Continue stitching all around and back to the beginning side. Leave a 12" or larger opening. Clip corners to reduce excess. Turn right side out through the opening. Slipstitch the opening closed by hand. The quilt may now be quilted by hand or machine.

The disadvantage to this method is that once the edges are sewn in, any creases or wrinkles that might form during the quilting process cannot be flattened out. Tying is the preferred method for finishing a quilt constructed using this method.

Bringing the backing fabric to the front is another way to finish the quilt's edge without binding. To accomplish this, complete the quilt as for hand or machine quilting. Trim the batting only even with the front. Trim the backing 1" larger than the completed top all around.

Turn the backing edge in ½" and then turn over to the front along edge of batting. The folded edge may be machine-stitched close to the edge through all layers, or blind-stitched in place to finish.

The front may be turned to the back. If using this method, a wider front border is needed. The backing and batting are trimmed 1" smaller than the top and the top edge is turned under ½" and then turned to the back and stitched in place.

One more method of self-finish may be used. The top and backing may be stitched together by hand at the edge. To accomplish this, all quilting must be stopped ½" from the quilt-top edge. The top and backing of the quilt are trimmed even and the batting is trimmed to ¼"–½" smaller. The edges of the top and backing are turned in ¼"–½" and blind-stitched together at the very edge.

These methods do not require the use of extra fabric and save time in preparation of binding strips; they are not as durable as an added binding.

Binding. The technique of adding extra fabric at the edges of the quilt is called binding. The binding encloses the edges and adds an extra layer of fabric for durability.

To prepare the quilt for the addition of the bind-

ing, trim the batting and backing layers flush with the top of the quilt using a rotary cutter and ruler or shears. Using a walking-foot attachment (sometimes called an even-feed foot attachment), machine-baste the three layers together all around approximately ⅛" from the cut edge.

Bias binding may be purchased in packages and in many colors. The advantage to self-made binding is that you can use fabrics from your quilt to coordinate colors. Double-fold, straight-grain binding and double-fold, bias-grain binding are two of the most commonly used types of binding.

Double-fold, straight-grain binding is used on smaller projects with right-angle corners. Double-fold, bias-grain binding is best suited for bed-size quilts or quilts with rounded corners.

To make double-fold, straight-grain binding, cut 2¼"-wide strips of fabric across the width or down the length of the fabric totaling the perimeter of the quilt plus 10". The strips are joined as shown in **Figure 16** and pressed in half wrong sides together along the length using an iron on a cotton setting with no steam.

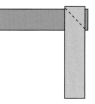

FIGURE 16 Join binding strips in a diagonal seam to eliminate bulk as shown.

Lining up the raw edges, place the binding on the top of the quilt and begin sewing (again using the walking foot) approximately 6" from the beginning of the binding strip. Stop sewing ¼" from the first corner, leave the needle in the quilt, turn and sew diagonally to the corner as shown in **Figure 17**.

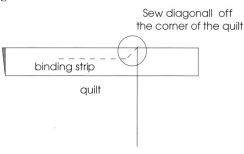

FIGURE 17 Sew to within ¼" of corner; leave needle in quilt, turn and stitch diagonally off the corner of the quilt.

Fold the binding at a 45-degree angle up and away from the quilt as shown in **Figure 18** and back down flush with the raw edges. Starting at the top raw edge of the quilt, begin sewing the next side as shown in **Figure 19**. Repeat at the next three corners.

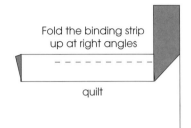

FIGURE 18 Fold binding at a 45-degree angle up and away from quilt as shown.

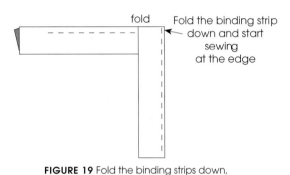

FIGURE 19 Fold the binding strips down, flush with the raw edge, and begin sewing.

As you approach the beginning of the binding strip, stop stitching and overlap the binding ½" from the edge; trim. Join the two ends with a ¼" seam allowance and press the seam open. Reposition the joined binding along the edge of the quilt and resume stitching to the beginning.

To finish, bring the folded edge of the binding over the raw edges and blind-stitch the binding in place over the machine-stitching line on the backside. Hand-miter the corners on the back as shown in **Figure 20**.

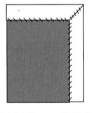

FIGURE 20 Miter and stitch the corners as shown.

If you are making a quilt to be used on a bed, you may want to use double-fold, bias-grain bindings because the many threads that cross each other

along the fold at the edge of the quilt make it a more durable binding.

Cut 2¼"-wide bias strips from a large square of fabric. Join the strips as illustrated in Figure 16 and press the seams open. Fold the beginning end of the bias strip ¼" from the raw edge and press. Fold the joined strips in half along the long side, wrong sides together, and press with no steam (**Figure 21**).

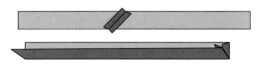

FIGURE 21 Fold and press strip in half.

Follow the same procedures as previously described for preparing the quilt top and sewing the binding to the quilt top. Treat the corners just as you treated them with straight-grain binding.

Since you are using bias-grain binding, you do have the option to just eliminate the corners if this option doesn't interfere with the patchwork in the quilt. Round the corners off by placing one of your dinner plates at the corner and rotary-cutting the gentle curve (**Figure 22**).

FIGURE 22 Round corners to eliminate square-corner finishes.

As you approach the beginning of the binding strip, stop stitching and lay the end across the beginning so it will slip inside the fold. Cut the end at a 45-degree angle so the raw edges are contained inside the beginning of the strip (**Figure 23**). Resume stitching to the beginning. Bring the fold to the back of the quilt and hand-stitch as previously described.

FIGURE 23 End the binding strips as shown.

Overlapped corners are not quite as easy as rounded ones, but a bit easier than mitering. To make overlapped corners, sew binding strips to opposite sides of the quilt top. Stitch edges down to finish. Trim ends even.

Sew a strip to each remaining side, leaving 1½"–2" excess at each end. Turn quilt over and fold binding down even with previous finished edge as shown in **Figure 24**.

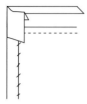

FIGURE 24 Fold end of binding even with previous page.

Fold binding in toward quilt and stitch down as before, enclosing the previous bound edge in the seam as shown in **Figure 25**. It may be necessary to trim the folded-down section to reduce bulk.

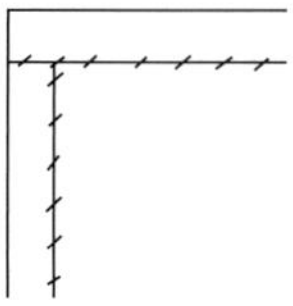

FIGURE 25 An overlapped corner is not quite as neat as a mitered corner.

Final Touches

If your quilt will be hung on the wall, a hanging sleeve is required. Other options include purchased plastic rings or fabric tabs. The best choice is a fabric sleeve, which will evenly distribute the weight of the quilt across the top edge, rather than at selected spots where tabs or rings are stitched, keep the quilt hanging straight and not damage the batting.

To make a sleeve, measure across the top of the finished quilt. Cut an 8"-wide piece of muslin equal to that length—you may need to seam several muslin strips together to make the required length.

Fold in ¼" on each end of the muslin strip and press. Fold again and stitch to hold. Fold the muslin strip lengthwise with right sides together. Sew along the long side to make a tube. Turn the tube right side out; press with seam at bottom or centered on the back.

Hand-stitch the tube along the top of the quilt and the bottom of the tube to the quilt back making sure the quilt lies flat. Stitches should not go through to the front of the quilt and don't need to be too close together as shown in **Figure 26**.

FIGURE 26 Sew a sleeve to the top back of the quilt.

Slip a wooden dowel or long curtain rod through the sleeve to hang.

When the quilt is finally complete, it should be signed and dated. Use a permanent pen on the back of the quilt. Other methods include cross-stitching your name and date on the front or back or making a permanent label which may be stitched to the back.

Special Thanks

We would like to thank the talented quilt designers whose work is featured in this collection.

Betty Alderman
T Is for Tulips, 106

Pat Campbell
Chained Lightning, 82
Floating Triangles Wall Quilt, 118

Barbara Clayton
Irish Dresden Plate, 51
My Dinosaur Baby, 10
Spooky Halloween, 123

Sue Harvey
Sunlit Scraps, 70

Sandra Hatch
Scrappy Prairie Queen, 35

Paula Jeffery
Embroidered Blocks Baby Quilt, 6

Connie Kauffman
Denim Table Runner, 101
Polka Dot Party, 32
Triangle Plaids, 143

Pearl Louise Krush
Autumn Ridge Lap Quilt, 146
Star-Spangled Scrap Quilt, 38

Chris Malone
Farm Animal Baby Quilt, 16

Connie Rand
Random Colors, 46

Jill Reber
Here a Chick, There a Chick, 22
Mosaic Memories, 150

Judith Sandstrom
Diamonds on Parade, 43
Field of Diamonds, 62
Purple Passion, 67

Christine Schultz
Which Way Home?, 79

Carla Schwab
Four Seasons, 160

Marian Shenk
Bed of Lilies, 96
Flower Garden Square, 91

Ruth Swasey
Civil War Notes to Home, 154
Crazy Eights, 157
Squares & Triangles, 135

Rhonda Taylor
Crazy About Jingleberries, 111
Plaid Jubilee, 86

Jodi Warner
Christmas Counterchange, 58
Road Crew Rally, 27

Julie Weaver
Blueberries & Cream, 74
Tic-Tac-Toe, 139

Bea Yurkerwich
Song of Spring, 131

Fabrics & Supplies

Page 22: Here a Chick, There a Chick—Master Piece 45 ruler and Static Stickers and Pfaff sewing machine.

Page 32: Polka Dot Party--Sulky variegated thread.

Page 35: Scrappy Prairie Queen—Fairfield Processing Classic Cotton batting and Star Machine Quilting Thread from Coats.

Page 62: Field of Diamonds—Hobbs Heirloom Premium cotton batting, Fiskars rotary-cutting tools, Steam-A-Seam from The Warm Co., and DMC quilting thread and needles.

Page 67: Purple Passion—Hobbs Heirloom Premium cotton batting, Fiskars rotary-cutting tools and DMC quilting thread and needles.

Page 74: Blueberries & Cream—Warm & Natural cotton batting.

Page 123: Spooky Halloween—Heat 'n Bond Ultrahold no-sew fusible web.

Page 143: Triangle Plaids—Hobbs Heirloom Fusible Batting and Signature machine-quilting thread.

Page 146: Autumn Ridge Lap Quilt—Warm & Natural cotton batting.